FontFace

Commissioning Editor: Isheeta Mustafi
Art Director: Emily Portnoi
Art Editor: Jennifer Osborne
Design Concept: Emily Portnoi
Design: Filthy Media

First published 2012
by Focal Press
70 Blanchard Road, Suite 402, Burlington, MA 01803

Focal Press is an imprint of the Taylor & Francis Group,
an informa business

Library of Congress Cataloging in Publication Data
A catalog record for this book has been requested

ISBN: 9780240823973

FontFace

THE COMPLETE GUIDE TO CREATING,
MARKETING, AND SELLING DIGITAL FONTS

ALEC JULIEN

Focal Press
Taylor & Francis Group

Table of Contents

1

Typography Essentials   10

2

Creating A Font   42

3

Going Pro 170

4

Resources 192

Introduction

There are two germinal typographic moments in my life that stand out like 72-point swashes on the pages of my memory.

When I was a youngster during the pre-PC Stone Age, my mother brought home a wonderful electric typewriter. It featured a magical sphere of glyphs that, upon the striking of a key, would rotate to the appropriate letter and strike an inky ribbon against the paper. It was a marvel of engineering, but the genuinely magical thing about this sphere was that it was swappable with other spheres; and these other spheres had differently shaped letters on them. It was the first time I realized what a font was.

Fast forward to my graduate school days. PCs were ubiquitous by then, and fonts were available by the dozens on even a vanilla installation of any operating system and word-processing package. After experimenting with as many fonts as I could get my hands on, I became obsessed with finding the perfect text font for scholarly work.

I perused, hunted, and otherwise researched what was out there as best I could, settling eventually on some variety of Garamond that I knew I was destined to leave behind someday for a prettier face. And then one day a small pamphlet from Adobe arrived in my mailbox. And within its lovely pages sat my holy grail: a sample of the font Minion.

I'll never forget that first look at what struck me as perfection in type design: unflawed construction and balance, unmatched synergy between glyphs, beauty that was also entirely readable. Upon acquiring a copy of the font and feeling far superior to my typographically stunted classmates, I was put in my place by my institution: the instructions given to me for writing my thesis explicitly stated that the use of any other font besides Times New Roman had to be approved by some sort of committee of robe-wearing, incanting administrators. Spinelessly, I used Times New Roman.

The experience taught me two things: first, that I was determined to be braver in the future as an agent of typographic knowledge and change; and, second, that someday I would create my own fonts, perhaps even something as lovely as Minion. I have made many fonts (some samples of which you can see here); I still haven't made my Minion. But what I have done is to teach myself quite a lot about how to create fonts, and quite a lot about fonts and typography in general. This book is the book I wish that I had when I first started creating fonts—a guide through the basics of fonts and the nitty-gritty of the font creation process. I hope it helps some of you create your Minions.

AJHand

AJHand was the first font I created (in 2007), and it's my own handwriting. I had originally planned it to be a font used just for chord symbols for jazz and pop music charts, but I thought it looked good enough to develop into a general-purpose face.

Blues City

Blues City was based on neon signage for a restaurant I stumbled across. It was one of those fonts with which I had to balance the need for a nearly infinite supply of ligatures with the finite amount of time in the universe. I managed to make 700 glyphs overall.

HUNK

HUNK WAS THE FIRST ALL-CAPS FONT I CREATED. I FELT A LITTLE GUILTY RELEASING A FONT WITHOUT ANY LOWERCASE GLYPHS, BUT EVERY ATTEMPT I MADE TO CREATE A LOWERCASE FELT ARTIFICIAL, SO I RELEASED IT AS WAS.

M7

M7 was my third experiment with slab serifs and my first font with a successful light weight.

Joules

I created Joules in 2007, a few months after AJHand. It's another font based on my own handwriting, but I wanted it a little more upright and legible than AJHand.

7

How to use this book

The purpose of this book is to walk you through the entire font design process, from the first moments of inspiration through to marketing and selling your finished fonts. We have included a few features in this book to help you get the most from this information.

TUTORIAL RATINGS

Each step-by-step tutorial has been given a difficulty level rating, indicated by the icon at the top of the page.

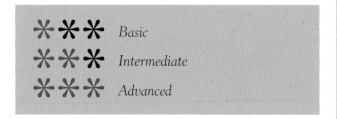

✳ ✳ ✳ *Basic*
✳ ✳ ✳ *Intermediate*
✳ ✳ ✳ *Advanced*

COLOR CODING

Each page features a key color that lets you know at a glance whether that page includes information about a particular software program or is software "neutral."

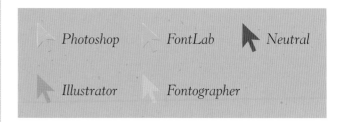

Photoshop *FontLab* *Neutral*

Illustrator *Fontographer*

TYPES OF PAGE

Section Openers—as well as listing what's coming up in the following chapters, the Section Openers suggest alternative ways for working your way through the book by suggesting where you can jump from one subject to another, if you wish.

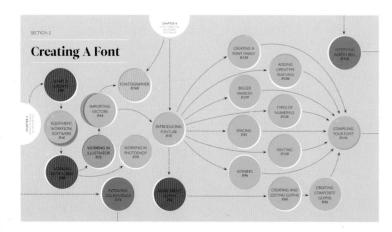

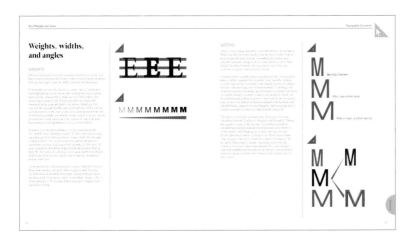

Information Pages—these pages provide an overview of a particular subject. Color coding signals which type of information is covered. Each image has a number that is referred to in the text.

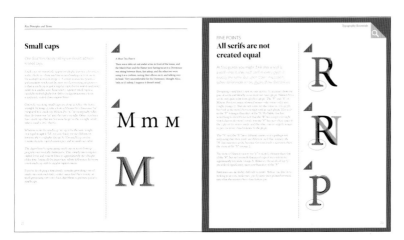

Fine Points—these sidebars appear throughout the book and add a little extra to your font knowledge. Color coding signals the beginning of the sidebar. The information in each Fine Point is self-contained, so does not follow on from the pages around it.

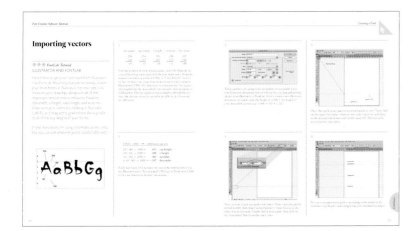

Tutorials—these pages provide step-by-step instructions for designing digital fonts. Icons indicate the level of difficulty of the tutorial.

Typography Essentials

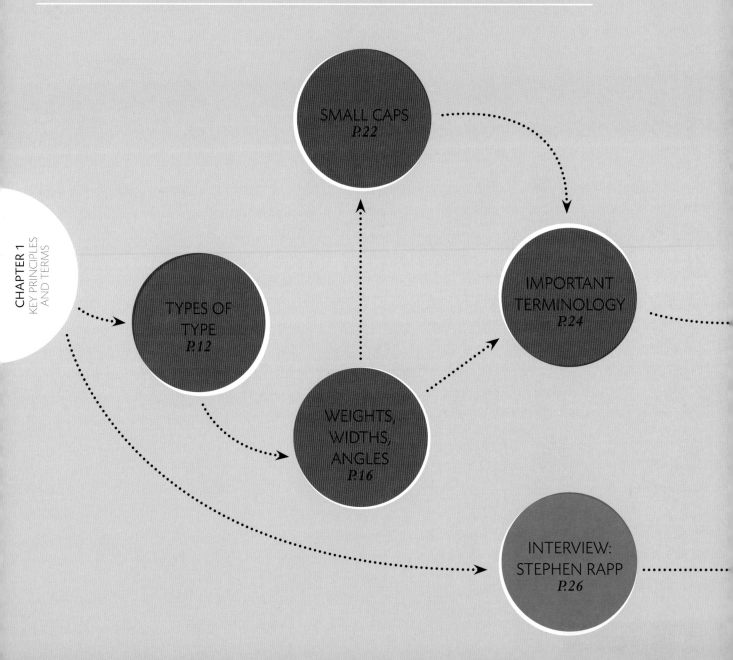

CHAPTER 1
KEY PRINCIPLES
AND TERMS

SMALL CAPS
P.22

TYPES OF
TYPE
P.12

WEIGHTS,
WIDTHS,
ANGLES
P.16

IMPORTANT
TERMINOLOGY
P.24

INTERVIEW:
STEPHEN RAPP
P.26

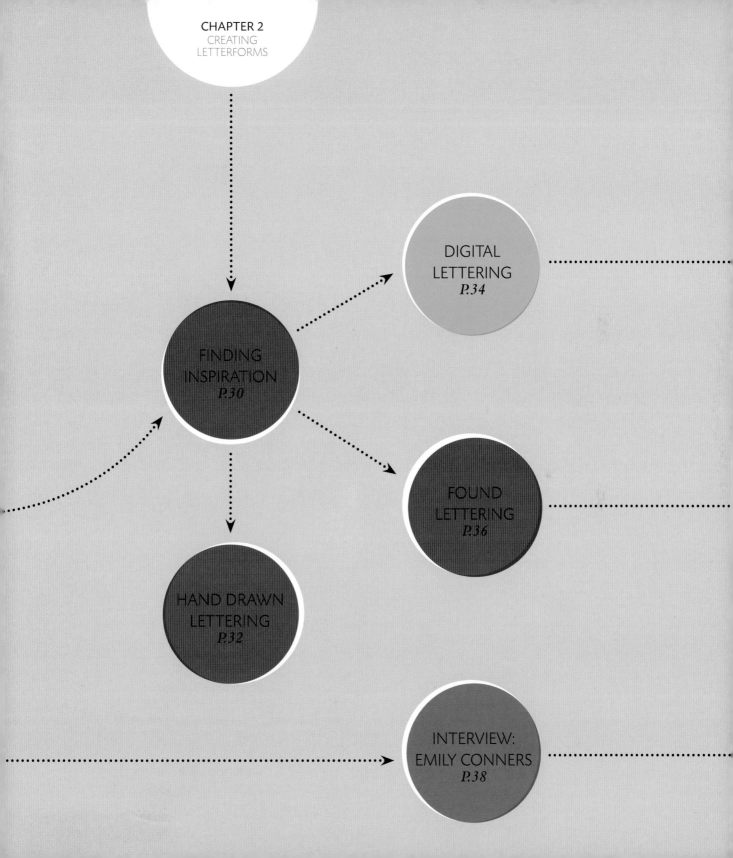

Types of type

This book is not meant to serve as a comprehensive reference for type classification and analysis. However, a brief examination of some of the major categories of typefaces will serve us well as we think about the font creation process.

Let's start off as basically as we can. The least fine-grained distinction to be made in type design is between serif and sans serif typefaces. To introduce the distinction visually, I'll trot out two of my favorite fonts, workhorses of typography: Minion and Frutiger (image 1).

The defining characteristic of a serif typeface is, naturally, the serif. "Serif" is one of those words that's easier to grasp visually than to define soundly, but something like "the little feet at the bottoms and tops of letters" gets at it fairly well (this is highlighted in image 2).

Fonts without serifs are called "sans serif" fonts ("sans" meaning "without" in French). In image 1, Minion is a serif font, and Frutiger is a sans serif. Serif fonts are traditionally used in large tracts of printed text. Some people have claimed that scientific research proves that serif faces are easier to read in such circumstances. There are still debates on the subject, but if you're typesetting a book or an essay, a serif font will generally be called for. Sans serif fonts are typically used in less densely worded typographic applications—headlines, short runs of text in posters, callouts, and the like.

One basic rule of thumb to grasp is this: historically, serif fonts are calligraphic in nature. That is, the width of their strokes varies, as if someone were drawing each letter with a calligraphic pen with a wide, flat nib. Many sans serif fonts, on the other hand, are closer to being monoline; that is, their strokes are relatively fixed-width (this is highlighted in image 3).

Garamond

Baskerville

Didot

Rockwell

SERIF FONTS

Depending on who you ask, there are many classifications within the genre of serif fonts. I will touch on only four here, since these four demonstrate a very relevant distinction in font creation. The classifications are (in historical order of invention):

Old style—old-style fonts feature a non-vertical axis (the thinnest and thickest parts of the letters' strokes are slightly off-center, as if drawn by hand at a small oblique angle to the paper), as well as a low calligraphic contrast between thicker and thinner stroke parts. (See Garamond above.)

Transitional—transitional fonts have a greater contrast between thicker and thinner strokes, and often a more vertical axis than their old-style counterparts. (See Baskerville above.)

Modern—modern fonts sport a huge contrast between strokes, as well as thin serifs, and perfectly vertical axes. (See Didot above.)

Slab—slab serif fonts generally have very little contrast between thick and thin strokes, and have thick rectangular serifs. (See Rockwell above.)

Helvetica

Gill Sans

Futura

SANS SERIF FONTS

Sans serif fonts can, for our purposes, be divided into three broad categories:

Grotesque—rumor has it that the label "grotesque" was applied to the first widespread incarnations of sans serif fonts simply because they were so plain that purists were rather disgusted by them. Whatever the case, grotesque (sometimes referenced as "grotesk," and I am also lumping in the category neo-grotesque as well as gothic here) fonts are stark examples of minimalist aesthetics. (See Helvetica above.)

Humanist—to fix the issue that some people had with the grotesqueness of grotesque fonts, designers started to add some warm, "humanist" characteristics to their sans serif fonts, such as greater variations in stroke widths, designing with ovals instead of circles, and a slightly more delicate appearance. (See Gill Sans above.)

Geometric—geometric fonts are modeled upon perfect geometric figures, and feature a very clean, sturdy aesthetic. (See Futura above.)

Continues...

Suomi Hand

Alpine Script

Breath Pro

SCRIPT FONTS

And now to throw the third major classification into the mix of types of type: script fonts. These run the gamut from informal handwriting to formal scripts, and we can divide them into three broad categories:

Handwriting—handwriting fonts are meant to capture an individual's actual handwriting. They are great for informal presentations of concepts. (See Suomi Hand above.)

Brush script—brush script fonts are meant to reflect an artisan's affected handwriting for display purposes, as if drawn by a skilled sign painter with a brush. They are good for large, attention-grabbing applications such as posters and signs. (See Alpine Script above.)

Formal script—formal script fonts are meant to be carefully crafted calligraphic masterpieces. They are perfect for invitations, awards, and product packaging. (See Breathe Pro above.)

Script fonts are all meant to appear as if they were drawn by hand, ranging from less to more careful and precise calligraphers—handwriting faces appear as if they were just dashed off in a casual moment; brush scripts as if they were drawn by an extremely practiced hand that doesn't need to take great care to make something lovely; and formal scripts as if they were drawn by an extremely practiced, patient, and precise calligrapher.

OTHER FONT CATEGORIES

These three categories—serif, sans serif, and script—and their respective sub-categories, while very useful for our purposes, are not exhaustive, mutually exclusive, or prescriptive. You could have (and there do exist), for instance, more calligraphically weighted sans serif fonts, and serif handwriting fonts. But when you're deciding what sort of font to create, you should bear in mind these general classifications, since they might help direct you in choosing a design on which to work, and at the very least help you to talk about your fonts once it's time to market them.

And, yes, I realize I'm neglecting some font categories. There are display fonts—fonts that are meant to be used at large sizes in visually arresting applications; there are monospaced fonts—fonts that are often used by computer programmers for easy screen reading—and their cousin category of typewriter fonts. There are blackletter, Art Deco, grunge, comic book, bitmap, and hundreds of other categories. However, if you look at the samples of each of these fonts in image 1, you can generally distill each font down to one or a combination of the three categories addressed above.

DISPLAY

cuadrifonte, sans serif, handwriting

monospaced

andale mono, sans serif

typewriter

american typewriter, serif

Blackletter

aeronaut plain, formal script

ART DECO

lockwood, sans serif

Grunge

spud af tatty, sans serif

COMIC BOOK

hometown hero bb, sans serif, brush script

BITMAP

visitor tt1 brk, sans serif

Weights, widths, and angles

WEIGHTS

Often a font family (from the categories detailed previously) will have several related members in it. Some of these family members will vary by weight, some by width, and some by slant angle.

Font weights are an easy concept to grasp—we are all familiar with highlighting text in our favorite word-processing program, and pressing command-b to make our text bold. Some word-processing programs will, if they can't find an actual bold version of a font, generate their own version of bold text for you, but this algorithmically generated bold text will be inferior in most respects to the text produced by a handcrafted bold font. So whenever possible, you should design not just a regular version of a font, but a bold version as well, so users of your font don't have to rely on bad algorithms to see your font bolded.

In image 1, on the left is Minion's "E" in its regular weight. The middle shows Minion's regular "E" after a word-processing algorithm got hold of it and tried to make it bold. On the right is Minion Bold's "E"—a much more beautiful bold than the algorithmic version. Applying a bold algorithm to Minion's "E" gives us a drastically different glyph from the genuine Minion Bold "E." The stem of each glyph is the same width, but Minion Bold's horizontal bars are much thinner than the algorithm's pseudo-bold ones.

A font needn't be content with just a regular and a bold version. Many font families will sport other weights as well. You may see fonts labeled ultrathin, thin, light, regular, normal, roman, medium, book, bold, heavy, black, or ultrablack. Image 2 shows Neue Helvetica's "M" in eight different weights, ranging from ultra thin to black.

WIDTHS

There is also a range of widths that a font family can encompass. When included in a font family, there are three widths that are most frequently used: narrow (or condensed), regular, and extended (or wide). Image 3 shows some members of the font family Akzidenz Grotesk, shown in (from top to bottom) condensed, regular, and extended versions.

A narrow font is artfully compressed horizontally. An extended font is artfully expanded horizontally. I say "artfully" in both cases because it most certainly is not simply a matter of taking the font and squeezing each character inward, or pulling each character outward. Creating a good narrow or extended font from its regular sibling is a complex task, some details of which will be touched upon in later chapters of this book. In the meantime, take a look at the difference between a handcrafted narrow and extended font, compared to what happens when a regular font is simply expanded or contracted horizontally (image 4).

The figures on the left of image 4 are, from top to bottom, Akzidenz Grotesk Condensed, Regular, and Extended. Taking the regular version as the baseline, the condensed and the extended have been handcrafted to represent characteristics of the family while being narrower and wider in each case. In the right-hand column of image 4, the black figures show what happens when you extend and contract the regular "M" in Adobe Illustrator, by simply expanding/narrowing the character in a strictly horizontal fashion. The color figures over-and underlaid on the right are the actual condensed and extended characters of the font from the left column, shown for contrast.

3

M
Mary had a little lamb

M
Mary had a little lamb

M
Mary had a little lamb

4

Continues…

Of course, one need not create an entire font family in order to talk about a single font's width. A single font can be labeled or thought of as narrow, regular, or extended, with or without related family members to round out the group. For example, Press Gothic Pro is available only in its arguably narrow form (top of image 5), and Flatiron ITC Std is available only its obviously wide form (bottom of image 5).

A point about readability: generally speaking, a narrow font will be less readable at small sizes than a regular or extended font. The converse is not necessarily true, but if you have a large headline, it might be easier to take in at a glance if it is set in a narrow font.

In image 6, I've set the type in the top example contrary to standard practice. The headline is set in a somewhat wide font, and the body text is set in a very narrow font. At 8 point, the narrow font is quite difficult to read, and at 28 point the wider font is disproportionately taking up too much horizontal space. In contrast, the type in the bottom example is set in a fairly standard way: condensed type for the headline, and wider type for the small print that follows. The body text, even at this small size, is quite readable because of its extra width. The headline is readable because even though the font is narrow, it is set at an appropriate size. These are important points to keep in mind when setting out to create a font. If, for instance, you're creating a narrow font, you should expect people to use it at relatively large sizes, and you should plan accordingly—small details will stand out at large sizes, and so you should be careful to craft your characters with this in mind.

Narrow type is great at large sizes

WIDE TYPE IS GREAT AT LARGE SIZES

Alice in Wonderland

Alice was beginning to get very tired of sitting by her sister on the bank, and of having nothing to do: once or twice she had peeped into the book her sister was reading, but it had no pictures or conversations in it, 'and what is the use of a book,' thought Alice 'without pictures or conversation?'

So she was considering in her own mind (as well as she could, for the hot day made her feel very sleepy and stupid), whether the pleasure of making a daisy-chain would be worth the trouble of getting up and picking the daisies, when suddenly a White Rabbit with pink eyes ran close by her.

Alice in Wonderland

Alice was beginning to get very tired of sitting by her sister on the bank, and of having nothing to do: once or twice she had peeped into the book her sister was reading, but it had no pictures or conversations in it, 'and what is the use of a book,' thought Alice 'without pictures or conversation?'

So she was considering in her own mind (as well as she could, for the hot day made her feel very sleepy and stupid), whether the pleasure of making a daisy-chain would be worth the trouble of getting up and picking the daisies, when suddenly a White Rabbit with pink eyes ran close by her.

ANGLES

Another way to add a new member to a font family is by varying its regular slant angle. Italic fonts are generally slanted at around 12° to the right from their regular siblings. Oblique fonts are similarly slanted; what distinguishes an italic font from an oblique font is that the italic version is generally not only slanted but also flourished.

In image 7, the characters in the left-hand column are Minion Pro's regular "o" and "b," while the magenta characters in the middle column are the same characters that have been slanted 12° to the right. (Note that there is no such font as Minion Pro Oblique, but if there were, this is what it would look like.) The characters in the right-hand column are the Minion Pro Italic "o" and "b." Note the differences: even in the "o," where no flourishes are added to the italic version, there is still a significant design difference between the italic and the oblique. Most strikingly, the italic version is slightly condensed.

The top row of text in image 8 shows Minion Pro on the left and Minion Pro Italic on the right. The bottom row shows Helvetica on the left and Helvetica Oblique on the right. Both the italic and oblique font are slanted at close to the same angle from their regular siblings, but the Minion Pro Italic font is also substantially redesigned.

The Minion Pro Italic "l" in image 8 is not merely slanted to the right, but also has curled ends where the serifs were. The Minion Pro Italic "a" in the example has gone from a two-story affair to a one story. These are typical italic maneuvers. Generally, serif font families employ genuine italics while sans serif font families often have simpler oblique siblings.

Oblique fonts are simply tilted without changing any essential characteristics of the regular version of the font. The Helvetica Oblique "l" and "a" are just tilted without added flourishes or structural changes. Although sans serif fonts tend to have oblique versions as opposed to italic, sometimes they are called "italic" just for the sake of not introducing unfamiliar terms to the font-buying public. It's rare for a font family to have both an italic and an oblique version.

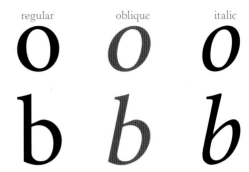

7

regular   oblique   italic

o   *o*   *o*

b   *b*   *b*

8

la → *la*
la → *la*

Continues...

ALL IN THE FAMILY

Say you were to develop a complete font family, with all variations of weight, width, and slant. Let's do the math, based on developing thin, regular, and bold weights, condensed, regular, and extended widths, and italics on top of everything. That would mean you'd have to develop the following fonts: thin condensed, thin condensed italic, thin regular, thin regular italic, thin extended, regular condensed, regular condensed italic, regular, italic, regular extended, regular extended italic, bold condensed, bold condensed italic, bold, bold italic, bold extended, and bold extended italic. That's 17 fonts to comprise the family. No small effort, but it could be a good selling point once you release your font family—designers like to be able to work with lots of well-crafted variations of a single font.

Of course, many fonts are released in just a single weight, width, and slant. For instance, many handwriting fonts come in only one variety, or a regular version and a bold at the most. It's rare for a handwriting font to sport more than two family members. Also many display and specialty fonts come in a single variety. Take a look at some examples in image 9.

It is not uncommon for a font family to have four members: regular, bold, italic, and bold italic; and in fact this is something for which you should aim if at all possible when developing a font. This covers all of your bases when a font user uses your font in a word-processing program—ctrl-b and ctrl-i and all of their combinations are set, and the word-processing program doesn't have to create pseudo-versions.

On the other hand, some font families come complete with dozens of family members. For instance, the lovely Gotham font family, by Hoefler & Frere-Jones, sports an impressive 66 family members, all centered around the mainstay of the family, Gotham Book—the "normal" version of Gotham from which its siblings take their basic form and familial traits. Futura, depending on which foundry's design you're looking at, has anywhere from 18 to 39 family members. Helvetica Neue sports 51 family members (image 10). Akzidenz Grotesk, depending again on which foundry's design you're looking at, has up to 39 family members, while Minion Pro has an impressive 65.

Luxus Brut has only one family member.

Marydale has three. (Regular, **bold**, & **black**.) That's a lot for a handwriting font family!

Hero has a light version along with the regular.

Tingle has a **bold version** along with the regular.

Helvetica Light
Helvetica Light Italic
Helvetica Roman
Helvetica Italic
Helvetica Medium
Helvetica Medium Italic
Helvetica Bold
Helvetica Bold Italic
Helvetica Heavy
Helvetica Heavy Italic
Helvetica Black
Helvetica Black Italic
Helvetica Thin Extended
Helvetica Thin Extended Oblique
Helvetica Ultra Light Extended
Helvetica Ultra Light Extended Oblique
Helvetica Extended
Helvetica Extended Oblique
Helvetica Medium Extended
Helvetica Medium Extended Oblique
Helvetica Bold Extended
Helvetica Bold Extended Oblique
Helvetica Heavy Extended
Helvetica Heavy Extended Oblique
Helvetica Black Extended
Helvetica Black Extended Oblique

Helvetica Thin Condensed
Helvetica Thin Condensed Oblique
Helvetica Ultra Light Condensed
Helvetica Ultra Light Condensed Oblique
Helvetica Light Condensed
Helvetica Light Condensed Oblique
Helvetica Condensed
Helvetica Condensed Oblique
Helvetica Medium Condensed
Helvetica Medium Condensed Oblique
Helvetica Bold Condensed
Helvetica Bold Condensed Oblique
Helvetica Black Condensed
Helvetica Black Condensed Oblique
Helvetica Extra Black Condensed
Helvetica Extra Black Condensed Oblique
Helvetica Thin
Helvetica Thin Italic
Helvetica Ultra Light
Helvetica Ultra Light Italic

Small caps

One final font family sibling we should address is small caps.

Small caps are essentially uppercase glyphs drawn at a lowercase scale, which are often used for section headings in text, as in the example shown in image 1. A common misconception—unfortunately reinforced by most word-processing programs—is that a small cap is just a regular capital letter scaled uniformly down to a smaller size. In actuality, a proper small cap is a carefully crafted glyph that differs in significant ways from a uniformly scaled-down capital letter.

Generally speaking, small caps are about as tall as the font's x-height. In image 2, take a look at Minion Pro's lowercase "m" compared to a small cap Minion Pro "m;" it's marginally taller than the lowercase "m" and the font's x-height. Other typefaces have small caps that are the same height as the x-height, while others stand a little shorter.

When we scale the small cap "m" up to be the same height as a regular capital "M", we can clearly see the differences between the two glyphs (image 3). The small cap version is wider than its capital counterpart and its serifs are taller.

The algorithms for generating small caps in most desktop programs are woefully inadequate. They simply take a regular capital letter and scale it down to approximately the x-height of the font, losing all the important, subtle differences between a real small cap and its regular capital cousin.

If you're developing a font family, consider providing a set of small caps with each font, so that users don't have to rely on word-processing software's bad algorithms to generate pseudo small caps.

A Mad Tea-Party

There was a table set out under a tree in front of the house, and the March Hare and the Hatter were having tea at it: a Dormouse was sitting between them, fast asleep, and the other two were using it as a cushion, resting their elbows on it, and talking over its head. 'Very uncomfortable for the Dormouse,' thought Alice; 'only, as it's asleep, I suppose it doesn't mind.'

FINE POINTS

All serifs are not created equal

At first glance, you might think that a serif is a serif—that is, that each serif in every glyph is exactly the same. But upon closer inspection, subtle differences across glyphs show themselves.

Designing a serif font is not an easy matter. You cannot draw one pair of serifs and blindly reuse them for every glyph. Minion Pro's serifs vary quite a bit from glyph to glyph. The "F" and "R" of Minion Pro have nearly identical stems—the same width and height (image 1). And the left serifs are the same in each glyph, but look at the stem's bottom-right serif in each glyph. The serif in the "F" is longer than that of the "R." Probably this has something to do with the fact that the "R" has a leg to the right that balances the stem's serifs; but the "F" has just white space to the right of the stem's serifs, and thus they can be slightly longer to provide more visual balance to the glyph.

The "N" and the "R" have different stems, so it's perhaps not surprising that their serifs are different, and that, namely, the "N" has narrower serifs, because the stem itself is narrower than the stem of the "R" (image 2).

The stem of Minion's lowercase "p" is slightly thinner than that of the "P", but not so much that you'd expect its serifs to be significantly less wide (image 3). However, the serifs of the "p" are indeed significantly narrower than that of the "P."

Serif fonts are devilishly difficult to create. Before you dive in to making your own, make sure you do some fine-pointed research into what the masters have done before you.

Important terminology

GLYPHS

I generally take "glyph" to mean an instantiated character ("a," "b," etc.) in your font editing software, although the term does have alternative meanings. For instance, in FontLab and Fontographer, the combined mark (or ligature) of "fl" is considered a glyph, while in many discussions outside of font creation, a ligature such as "fl" would be considered a fanciful rendering of two glyphs ("f" and "l") next to one another.

VERTICAL METRICS

The following terms can best be comprehended via the graphic shown in image 1.

Baseline—the imaginary line upon which the non-descending bottoms of glyphs sit.

Ascender—the imaginary line to which tall lowercase glyphs reach (e.g., "f," "b," "l," "h," "k").

Descender—the imaginary line that lowercase glyphs that fall below the baseline reach (e.g., "q," "y," "p," "j").

X-height—the imaginary line to which normally heighted lowercase glyphs reach (e.g., "w," "e," "r," "u," "o," "a," "s," "z," "x," "c," "v," "n," "m"). Notice that ascending and descending lowercase glyphs generally play well with a font's x-height; e.g., the loop of the "b" usually tops out at the x-height.

Cap height—the imaginary line to which uppercase glyphs reach (e.g., "f," "b," "l," "h," "k").

Overshoot—while the straight bottom of the "f" sits precisely on the baseline, the curved bottom of the "d" generally descends ever so slightly below the baseline. Creating this overshoot for rounded glyphs is standard practice in type design; the reason being that if the curved bottom of the "d" and the straight bottom of the "f" came exactly to the baseline, it would appear to the naked eye as if the "d" were smaller than the "f." This goes for any glyph rounded on the top or bottom. In image 2, the lines show the baseline, x-height, ascender, and the overshoots of curved glyphs from these vertical metrics.

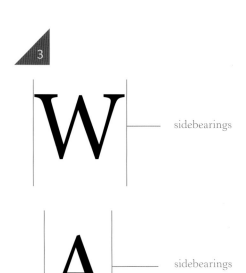

HORIZONTAL METRICS

Sidebearings—the imaginary lines that denote the left and right boundaries of a glyph. Without sidebearings, programs that use your fonts wouldn't know where a glyph begins and ends.

Kerning—you can make a font function fairly well with careful use of sidebearings, but even the best sidebearings won't be good enough to ensure proper letterspacing with every pair of glyphs. In image 3 we can see an example of good sidebearings for a "W" and an "A." But put these glyphs next to each other, and a visual problem arises. The solution is kerning—the process of providing instructions to your font on how to precisely handle spacing between problematic letter pairs. In image 4, we have some unkerned text on the left, set simply by relying on those proper sidebearings. On the right, is a sample of properly kerned text, where the "A" doesn't respect the "W" 's right sidebearing.

FURTHER TERMS

Here are some important anatomical terms, as shown in image 5:

Stem—the major vertical stroke in a glyph.

Counter—the open space in a fully or partly closed area within a glyph.

Lobe—a closed circular stroke in a glyph.

Leg—a diagonal offshoot stroke of a glyph, such as in an "R" or "K."

Diagonal—a major diagonal stroke of a glyph, such as in "A."

Crossbar—a horizontal stroke neither at the top nor the bottom of a glyph, which joins two other strokes, such as in "A" and "4."

Arm—a jutting horizontal stroke, such as in "E/F."

Ligature—two letterforms joined together to create a single form. The classic example is "f i". The dot of the "i" intrudes into the space of the "f"'s overhanging arch, so typographers created the "fi" ligature, which often dispenses with the dot and brings the crossbar of the "f" across to the top of the "i". There are two types of ligatures: standard and discretionary.

Hinting—the process of programming your font to display well at all sizes on electronic displays.

WATER IS VAPORIZING.   WATER IS VAPORIZING.

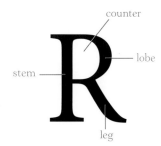

diagonal

crossbar

counter

stem

lobe

leg

arm

Stephen Rapp

Stephen Rapp has been a lettering artist for over 20 years. He was a recipient of the Hermann Zapf Scholarship Award in 1997 and has been a lettering artist and type developer for American Greetings since 2000.

Stephen's work has been exhibited in numerous publications including *Letter Arts Review*, *Scripsit*, *Bound and Lettered*, *Modern Mark Making* by Quarry Books, and *Typography 30* by The Type Directors Club. He has taught classes and workshops on both calligraphy and lettering and has been a faculty member at the International Lettering Arts Conference and Typecon.

In addition to his work with American Greetings, Stephen designs commercially available fonts for Fontshop, P22, Veer, and MyFonts.

How did you decide to create fonts?

"I had been interested in typography and calligraphy for many years. I did a lot of calligraphic art back then that incorporated type as well. In 1999 I showed a lettering sample of mine to Michael Clark, who is also a type designer. He convinced me to develop a font from the sample. That was my first font called Tai Chi."

Have you learned any lessons from creating fonts that you would share with a novice?

"I usually urge people to read up on forums like Typophile to get acquainted with the basics. Generally speaking, I don't recommend going into it for the money. Making fonts takes a lot of patience. It's more rewarding overall if you're doing it out of passion."

What is your font creation process?

"Most of my designs are scripts based on my own lettering (I spent over a decade lettering for the greeting card industry). I typically write out long passages of text to both clarify the style and to create a pool of letters. I scan the lettering and touch it up in Photoshop. Next I import characters into the background layer of FontLab Studio for drawing outlines. For more formal type, I usually draw just a few characters in pencil and do the rest directly in FontLab."

What are your thoughts about the future of the font business?

"I suspect the market for fonts will continue to expand. Back in the 1990s, when everyone was first starting to crank out type designs with Fontographer, there was a feeling that the market would get saturated. Given how fast design trends evolve and technology advances, I think the market is not likely to slow down much. Type for web and devices is in high demand. I do a lot of custom type myself and have had to create and alter fonts for very specific web applications. Marketing outlets for fonts have also made a lot of changes. It wasn't so long ago that huge foundries like Adobe and Linotype were where most everyone turned for type. Then a lot of small foundries popped up and now big retailers market for everyone from the major players to the one or two person microfoundry."

Do you remember the first time you saw a font of yours used on product packaging or a website?

"The first time I really recall was just minutes after talking about my first font, Tai Chi, with a friend. We walked into Applebees for lunch and it was on the menu. They had italicized it, but it looked fantastic. The font I see the most is Memoir. That's all over packaging at Trader Joe's, photography websites, book titles, and was even on a Taylor Swift CD. It's always a nice feeling to see something you've created out and about in the real world."

What are some of your favorite fonts by other designers?

"For the more elaborate renditions of American Penmanship, Ale Paul has raised the bar. Burgues Script is a great example of this. I like a lot of House Industry's work, particularly the Studio Lettering series. I also like Bello by Underware. It's fat and quirky, but has great impact."

Font creation can be a very solitary endeavor. Do you feel like it's important to connect with other font designers? What sorts of outlets are important along these lines?

"It is important. I used to work in-house at American Greetings. A design studio of that scale is rare and provides a lot of opportunity to learn and collaborate. Now that I'm on my own, I try to get out to conferences and workshops. I also connect through Facebook, email, and phone. I also teach, which I find both rewarding and a learning experience."

Do you formally copyright your fonts?

"No. I have a EULA (end user's license agreement). Supposedly the software is the only copyrightable part of a font design. So even if you get a copyright, anyone bent on profiting from your design can find a way around the actual copyright. I just do my best work and am happy that there are enough honest folks out there to make it worthwhile."

Where do you get inspiration?

"Everywhere! Design is so abundant and there are loads of blogs that feature every kind of lettering. I also doodle a lot. I keep a lot of drawing tools and a Pentel Colorbrush around whenever I have idle time. I'm not disciplined enough to keep up with my sketchbooks all that much, but I almost always have several spiral bound notebooks and legal pads full of sketches and doodles. So every now and then I go through and pull out the better ones."

Do you have a formal typographic education? Do you think in-depth typographic knowledge makes one a better font designer?

"I have no formal typographic training. I studied calligraphy for several years, but typography and type design I had to learn on my own. I admire a lot of the young students coming out of design programs with a fresh mind for type. Coming from a more old school background, I do see the importance of having some grounding in traditional typography, but I'm also aware of the danger of losing that creative edge if you're not open to new things."

Is there an aspect of the business of fonts that you hate? One you love?

"Most type designers have a bit of a love/hate relationship with the work. I love the creative parts of concepting and drawing. Inevitably you have to get through the endless finer details of outlines and hours of kerning to put it all together. I think keeping a bit of perspective in your view of the work helps though. It also helps to have several projects in various stages so you can break the work up."

"Making fonts takes a lot of patience. It's more rewarding overall if you're doing it out of passion."

How did you get such lovely handwriting?

"I base fonts on my own writing, but I've never actually had particularly lovely handwriting. When you have to do lettering for greeting cards eight hours a day for a living, you learn to write beautifully in a great variety of styles. The main difference is that it's not my default handwriting, like I would use to write a grocery list. I practiced calligraphy for years and learned to translate that into more casual styles that are heavily influenced by handwriting. I think that's one of the traits of greeting card lettering that is distinct from traditional calligraphy."

Stephen Rapp

1.

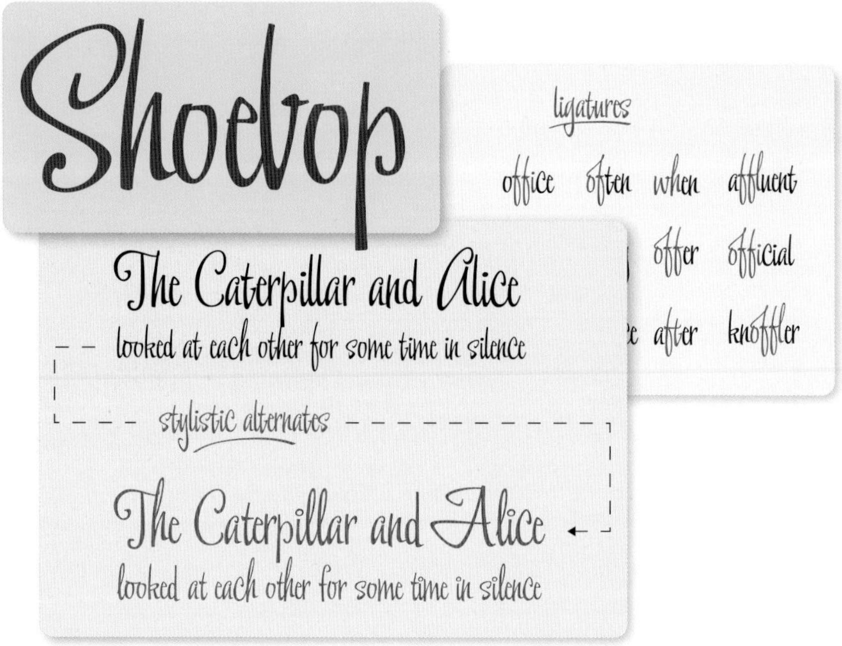

2.

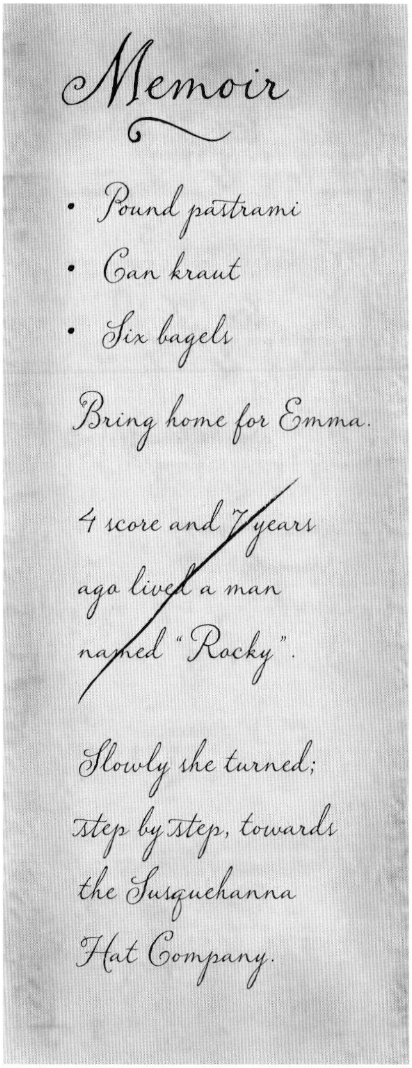

Shoefop

The Caterpillar and Alice
- - - looked at each other for some time in silence

- - - stylistic alternates - - -

The Caterpillar and Alice ←
looked at each other for some time in silence

ligatures

office   often   when   affluent

offer   official

after   knoffler

Memoir

- Pound pastrami
- Can kraut
- Six bagels

Bring home for Emma.

4 score and 7 years
ago lived a man
named "Rocky".

Slowly she turned;
step by step, towards
the Susquehanna
Hat Company.

3.

4.

Raniscript

It was a soft, misty day when Trenby called to drive Nan over to the Trevithick Kennels—one of those veiled mornings which break about noon into a glory of blue sky and golden sunlight. ❖

{ includes } *swashes* & **alternates**

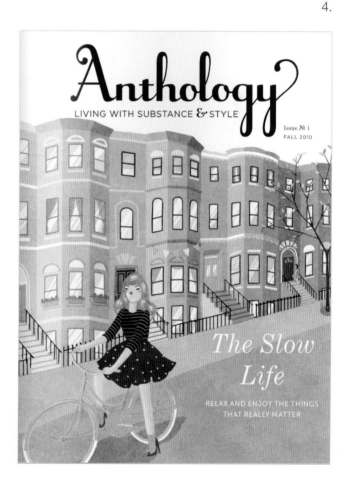

1. Shoebop: a playful, rhythmic brush script with a great retro flair.

2. Memoir: takes its inspiration from 18th-century handwritten letters, journals, and documents.

3. Raniscript: has an old-world feel with contemporary touches.

4. Raniscript: used for the masthead of *Anthology* magazine.

Chapter 2

CREATING LETTERFORMS

Finding inspiration

Now that some of the basics of the field are out of the way, we can get down to the business of creating fonts. And the first step toward creating a font is to come up with an interesting idea. Songwriters don't usually sit down with the vague plan to write a song—they generally have a genre in mind, and perhaps even an idea for a melodic line or a chord progression. Similarly, it will help you to have a genre of font in mind before starting to create one, and all the more so if you have an idea for a new twist or thematic element that will make your font unique.

Of course, there's nothing stopping you from sitting down, without any forethought, with the design software of your choice and just drawing letters. And occasionally this blank-canvas approach pays handsome dividends. But if you think about the font you're designing before you start designing it, you might be in a better position to come up with something cohesive and marketable.

One basic rule of thumb to grasp is this: historically, serif fonts are calligraphic in nature. That is, the width of their strokes varies, as if someone were drawing each letter with a calligraphic pen with a wide, flat nib. Many sans serif fonts, on the other hand, are closer to being monoline; that is, their strokes are relatively fixed-width.

FINDING A NICHE

So how do you find the inspiration to start developing a new font? One thing you can do is simply think about the fonts you've seen. (If you feel like you haven't seen many lately, you need to explore some font reseller sites, typography websites, magazines, and books—get neck deep in the fonts that are out there.) Is there a gap in the market that you think you could fill? There are thousands of handwriting fonts out there, but perhaps there are none that quite capture what your own handwriting does.

Or maybe you feel like there is a paucity of left-handed handwriting fonts on the market, and you're looking to contribute something lefty to the field. Perhaps you've experimented with a hundred sans serif families, but none strike you as professional while being somehow playful.

Maybe you've tried dozens of serif fonts for a book project, but you can't find one that is regal while being legible at small sizes. Perhaps you love slab serifs, but you find that most of them are a bit cold, and you'd like to try creating a friendlier slab. Maybe all of the narrow gothic headline fonts you've tried fail to wow you with details at 384 point. If you have done some due diligence with fonts that are already out there, and you've found a niche that needs attention, the chances are you're not alone, and the font you create to address the issue will be valuable to others as well.

PAYING HOMAGE

Alternatively, maybe you just have a burning desire to create something that's already been done, in which case market research be damned. If you aspire to create the next Minion or Helvetica, go for it. Chances are that by the end of the design process your font will be significantly original, even if it started as a homage to another face. No matter what you come up with in the end, the knowledge you'll gain by actually completing a font is vast and invaluable.

There are so many fonts out there that you might think discouragingly that everything has been done already. Then why should you bother? But I'm consistently surprised and delighted by new fonts that are introduced by font creators every day—somehow, there's always something new, some twist that no one has done before. Or, even if it's a twist that has been done before, somehow designers often find a way to work that twist in a unique way. At any rate, don't let a lack of originality stand in your way at the outset of creating a font. Throw some design against the wall and see what sticks.

YOUR FIRST PROJECT

Be forewarned: if this is your first foray into font design, diving right into a traditional serif typeface is a tall order. The subtleties of serif curves, brackets, thick/thin contrast, and axis tilt are many and varied, and it takes a skilled and knowledgeable font creator to instantiate all of these factors into an attractive face. So you might want to pick a sans serif or a handwriting font as your first project.

Hand-drawn lettering

One of the easiest (and most popular) ways to get inspired is by hand-drawn lettering. There's nothing quite like the beauty, originality, and variety of handwritten ink on paper. In Chapter 4 I'll be addressing the steps you'll take to turn handwriting on paper into a digital font, but for now let's talk about some of the nuances of types of handwritten type.

The easiest way to start a handwriting font is by using your own handwriting as a foundation—or that of someone you know with better penmanship! Image 1 shows a sample of my handwriting, which I used as the basis for my first font, AJHand (image 2). I have also designed a font called Zurdo, based on a friend's handwriting (image 3).

Issues to ponder at the outset, if you're going to be creating handwritten glyphs on paper, include the kind of paper to use (bright white is always best for the sake of contrast, but other factors include the paper's absorbency and texture), the kind of pen to use (calligraphic, ballpoint, marker, thick nib, thin nib, pencil), and the number of glyphs to put down on paper. Don't just draw "a" to "z" and expect that you're done.

In Chapter 4 we'll be going through the sorts of glyphs you should include in any font, but keep in mind for now that there are more than 26 characters, and there's nothing worse than having to go back months later to try to recreate some handwriting for the sake of getting more glyphs (believe me, I speak from experience). Forward thinking can save you a lot of headaches later. There are upper and lower cases, then there are numerals, accented glyphs, special characters, and non-Latin characters.

So your job of drawing glyphs on paper is more than just a few minutes' work. (FontLab does make life a bit easier than it would otherwise be. For instance, you don't have to draw "À," "È," "Ò," "Ù," separately from "A," "E," "O," and "U." As long as you have the accent mark—a "grave" in this instance—and the "A," "E," "O," and "U," FontLab and Fontographer make it easy to create accented versions of these glyphs in short order.)

If you're going to use someone else's handwriting as the basis of your font, then early on in the process you should discuss business arrangements with your handwriting muse. Will you pay her upfront for her handwriting samples? Will you give her a part of the font's future earnings? How long will the arrangement last?

When setting out to develop a handwriting font, keep in mind some of the distinctions from the previous chapter: will the handwriting be calligraphic or monoline, or somewhere in between? Where will it fall on the spectrum from handwriting to formal script? And keep in mind the following options as well. Will it have aspects of a grunge font (that is, will it show obvious signs of having been written on textured paper with an imperfect pen)? Will it be slanted or upright? Bold or fine? Do you think it will be feasible to have several different versions of the font—regular, bold, italic, and bold italic, for instance?

BORROWING INSPIRATION

Maybe your handwriting isn't particularly inspiring to you (though let me just say that of the thousands of handwriting fonts that are out there, many of them are not particularly interesting, and there's obviously a market for these fonts), and you don't know anyone else with particularly inspiring handwriting. All is not lost! Skip ahead to the section on Found Lettering (page 36) for ideas on how to borrow some inspiration from others!

2

AJHand

My very first font was based on my own handwriting. The process for creating a handwriting font like this will be detailed in an upcoming chapter.

3

Zurdo

This font is based on my friend's handwriting. It makes a lovely font, don't you think? (I thought she was left-handed when I first saw her writing, but she's not!)

Digital lettering

By "digital lettering" I mean the craft of sitting down at your computer and working directly with your design software to create glyphs from scratch. In the end, this will boil down to spending large chunks of your life in FontLab or Fontographer, and becoming well-versed in their tools. The bulk of the rest of this book will give you a taste of what this life is like.

Most of the fonts I have created have been drawn directly into FontLab (image 1). Sometimes I'll have an idea I'd like to explore; sometimes I'll just start drawing with FontLab's tools, and see what comes of it. More often than not, nothing good comes of it, and this is one lesson of digital lettering that you should learn straight away: don't be afraid to abandon a creation and start anew. For some people, it's far easier to throw away a piece of paper than a computer file, but to design a good font you have to be able to delete with impunity. Sometimes a bad start isn't worth the time it would take to fix it.

Another lesson that everyone in the digital age should be aware of, but which too few of us take seriously: save frequently and back up often! A digital font represents many, many hours of work, some of which may not be reproducible. You should always have a back-up copy of all of your digital files, preferably on a distant server that wouldn't go up in flames at the same time as your house. I use the Dropbox file-sharing service to back up my files immediately while I'm working on a new font, as well as an automated online back-up system to back up everything on my computer. And both systems have saved me on several occasions.

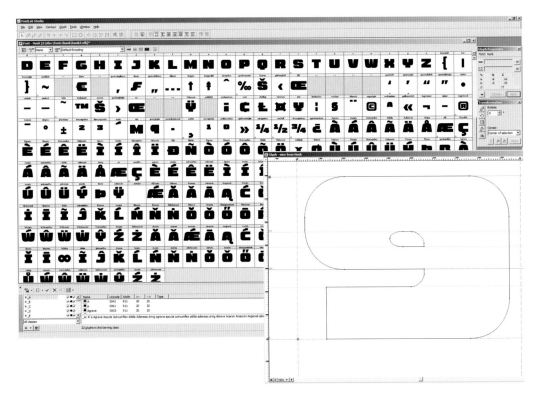

FINE POINTS

Junction heights

When I first started designing fonts, I thought, naively, that the junction points in the middle of the vertical bars of the "R," "P," "B," and "K" were all at the same height. Wouldn't it be easy if you could design a "P" and then just stick a leg on it for an "R," and another hoop on it for a "B"? I soon learned better. Font design is seldom this easy.

If you examine the mid-height junctions of several glyphs, in a variety of fonts, you see that there is a wide variety of heights at which they sit. The fonts in image 1 show the mid-height junctions in (from top to bottom) Myriad Pro, Toronto Subway, and Minion Pro.

Minion Pro's "A," "E," "F," "H," and "R" all have different mid-height junctions. What is the rhyme and reason behind the placement of these vertical junctions? It's all about visual balance. The crossbar of the "F" is lower than that of the "E" because the "E" has an arm on the baseline to help balance the glyph; the "F" on the other hand has nothing on the baseline except for serifs, and thus having the crossbar closer to the baseline helps the "F" balance its visual weight.

Similarly, Minion's "A" has a crossbar that is lower than the crossbar of the "H." If the "A" had a higher crossbar, it would look like it were about to fall over from being too top-heavy.

ABEFHKPRXY
ABEFHKPRXY
AEFHR

Found lettering

A wonderful source of typographic inspiration is to find samples of obscure and forgotten type in the world. Many of these untapped treasures are begging to be turned into a font by a motivated font creator such as yourself. Browse through online photography (there are entire groups on Flickr devoted to this), and search for pictures of old signs, books, posters, railway cars, and packaging materials. See what sparks your interest and keep an eye open for type treatments that you haven't seen before. They may not be entirely original, but if they're not in the public eye, there's a chance that you'll be creating a font that has few peers.

Some beautiful fonts have been created based on this sort of found inspiration; take a look at image 1 for some examples. Toronto Subway, a lovely geometric sans serif by David Vereschagin, was created based on the 1950s station identification and signage in the Toronto subway system. Luxus Brut, by Roland Hörmann, was inspired by a shop portal in Vienna. Geetype, by Nick Cooke, found its start in cigarette-pack lettering by A. M. Cassandre. Strangelove, by Marcus Sterz, was inspired by the credit lettering from the movie *Dr. Strangelove*. My own Doctor Cyclops was based upon a movie poster for the eponymous title; Yacht was brought to life via samples of 1930s hand-lettering for movie posters; and Blues City was inspired by a neon restaurant sign. Hot Streak PB, by Phil Bracco, was inspired by an old pulp-fiction paperback.

Of course, you should be careful and respectful of others' intellectual and artistic property—just because you see a type treatment in the world doesn't necessarily mean that it's OK to commandeer the design for your own font. There is a fuzzy line here that needs to be carefully navigated.

STRANGELOVE

Geetype

Luxus Brut

BLUES CITY

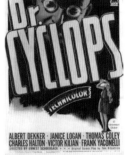

HOT STREAK PB

YACHT

Dr. CYCLOPS

Toronto Subway

Exercise due diligence—do your best to find out if this font has already been created. (If the nice, hand-drawn type you found on an old paperback turns out to be an actual font that was created to look like hand-drawn type—and the book you found isn't as old as you think it is—then you're going to be roundly embarrassed soon after you release your font and try to sell it.) If the font hasn't been created, but there are others very similar to it, make sure your version will have enough distinguishing characteristics to make it a useful addition to the world of fonts.

Sometimes, even the major players in the font industry don't respect this line. There are, for example, several versions of the Futura font from different foundries. (There are at least 10 versions—all extremely close to one another, and all called Futura—for sale on MyFonts.com at the time of writing.) There are fonts such as Eurostile and Frutiger that have been virtually cloned and given different names, Square721 and Humanist777 respectively (image 2). There are stories behind each of these cases, but the last thing you want, as an aspiring font creator, is to become embroiled in unnecessary intrigue. Err on the side of caution.

One gray area is something I call the "tracing exploit." The logic goes like this (and I am not a lawyer, so take what I say with the requisite grain of salt): a font is a digital file of nodes, curves, and code. This set of digital information is what can be protected under law—not the actual forms (concrete shapes) of the letters of the font—i.e., not the font's output. So if you take a font's output, stick a piece of tracing paper over it, copy the letterforms with a pencil, and then scan in "your" artwork and create a font out of it, there (so goes the tracing exploit's logic) is no legitimate conflict between your font and the one you traced. I don't ethically buy into this argument, but if you take your tracing paper, put it over a font's output, and commence to not tracing the actual letterforms, but creating a related but mutated version of the original font, I think you're potentially coming up with something quite unique, marketable, and not merely a clone. Search MyFonts.com for the term "sketch," and you'll see quite a few fonts that were created like this. For example, in image 3, Helvetica (top) was the inspiration for Sketchetik (bottom).

2

Eurostile is a lovely font

Square721 is a lovely font

Frutiger is a lovely font

Humanist777 is a lovely font

3

Helvetica

Helvetica

Emily Conners

Emily Conners is a self-taught type designer who started her own foundry, Emily Lime Design, in 2011.

She quickly released a handful of original fonts, along with the successful script Carolyna. Her work has been described as having "spontaneity, flow, quirkiness, and a lot of OpenType features to help make each typographic design unique and interesting."

Although mainly focused on creating new retail typefaces, Emily also makes time for custom lettering and design projects.

How did you get into typography in the first place?

"In probably the most unconventional way. My trained peers might be offended by my lack of typographic training, but I have a B.S. degree in Biology from the University of South Carolina. I worked in sales and management for 10 years and reached a point where I began to question my passion for the job. I started doing graphic design on the side to pay the bills, and that's when my love affair with type began."

Do you have a formal typographic education? Do you think in-depth typographic knowledge makes one a better font designer?

"No I don't, and yes, I do think in-depth knowledge makes for a better designer. I also know of other successful designers who are self taught, but you'd never know it, based on the quality of work they produce."

"I believe the future of the fonts business looks bright."

Do you remember the moment you decided you wanted to actually create a font? Looking back, once you started your first font, do you think you were well-prepared for the undertaking?

"Yes, distinctly. I can't remember what prompted me, but something made me think, "I CAN DO THIS." And I told my brother (who is more technically savvy than I) that we should do it together. But he didn't think I was serious. I was serious alright! Was I prepared? Absolutely not. But I was determined. I figured out FontLab and just went for it."

Any lessons learned from font creation that you'd share with a beginner?

"Well for me, I started with a fully-connected script font, so my lesson would be: DON'T do that. I had no idea what I was getting into. But my real advice would be to 'just go find the answers.' FontLab isn't easy, just go find the answers."

What is your font creation process?
Do you start with pencil and paper?
Draw glyphs in Illustrator?
Dive right into FontLab?

"My process varies depending on the style of font I want to create. When I want to create a handwritten font, I either start with a marker and paper, or I draw the glyphs directly in Illustrator. I refine my glyphs and once they are ready, I import them into FontLab. That's where the real fun begins."

Do you remember the first time
you saw one of your fonts used
by a designer? What was it?
How did it feel?

"Yes! Just recently I found my fonts on several blogs—and that was pretty exiting. I am still waiting to see them on a cover of a book or in a greeting card ... so if you see one, please tell me!"

"I figured out FontLab and just went for it."

Do you have any thoughts about
the future of the font business?
Is the current sales model a good one?
Can the industry support the increasing
number of designers and font releases
coming out? Will web fonts be a
continued factor in the future?

"I believe the future of the fonts business looks bright. There is a definite demand. So I believe an increase in the number of designers and designs can only lead to a positive overall effect. Good designers will be rewarded. And bad designs/designers will always be weeded out. Web fonts are definitely going to grow. I am curious to see how this plays out over the next few years."

How do you get inspiration
for your font designs?

"Calligraphy and lettering mostly."

What are some of your favorite
fonts from other designers?

"Oh I have so many! Graphik by Christian Schwartz, Mrs. Eaves from Emigre, Liza from Underware. I could come up with a list a mile long... I love so many!"

What's your favorite ligature?

"Livory's 'iv' ligature."

"I started doing graphic design on the side to pay the bills, and that's when my love affair with type began."

Is there an aspect of the business
of fonts that you hate? One you love?

"I hate kerning! Starting on a new font, though—that I love."

Emily Conners

1.

Emily Lime

Though Gorswen was the most quiet little country spot you could find, it lay only four miles away from Warford, a rising inland watering place, which boasted not only a Mayor and Corporation, but a pump-room and concert hall, and had a large and fleeting population of visitors and, to judge by its growing suburbs, an ever increasing number of residents.

Lilian and Peggy attended the Warford High School and Bobby the Grammar School. It was not quite what Father would have wished for them, for he had been a Rugby boy himself, but it was the best he could afford, and certainly the education was excellent, though the pupils were decidedly mixed. Still, as Aunt Helen said, 'You have no need to copy the manners of the children you meet. You have been taught at home to behave like gentlepeople, so please to remember you are Vaughans and keep up the credit of the family.'

Every morning at eight o'clock the little governess-car and Pixie, the steady black pony, stood ready at the side gate, and the trio jogged off to school with their lesson-books and their luncheons in their satchels [36] David could not be spared to go with them, but all the children had been taught to drive, and even Bobby had a firm hand on the reins, and knew the rules of the road as well as many a more experienced coachman, and I think, too, that Pixie had a sense of her responsibilities, and could be trusted not to get the wheel locked with a passing waggon, or to race too furiously down a steep hill, whatever feats her drivers might urge her to perform. The pony and trap were put up for the day at a quiet little inn midway between the two schools, and were always waiting

2.

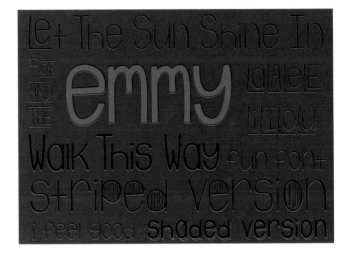

3.

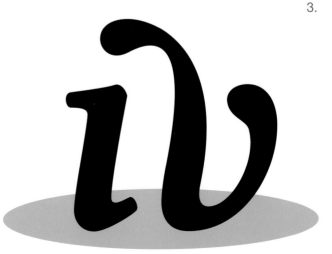

4.

5.

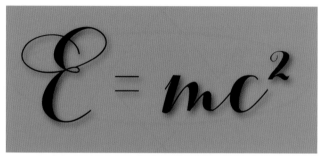

1. Carolyna Pro (headline) and Carolyna Pro Black (body text): elegant, yet whimsical handwritten calligraphic fonts created with readability in mind.

2. Emmy: samples from this family of fun handwriting fonts.

3. Livory: the "iv" ligature by HVD Fonts.

4. Revel: a stylish, distressed font that is both strong and delicate.

5. Carolyna Pro Black: with math glyphs.

Creating A Font

CHAPTER 4
FONT CREATION
SOFTWARE
TUTORIALS

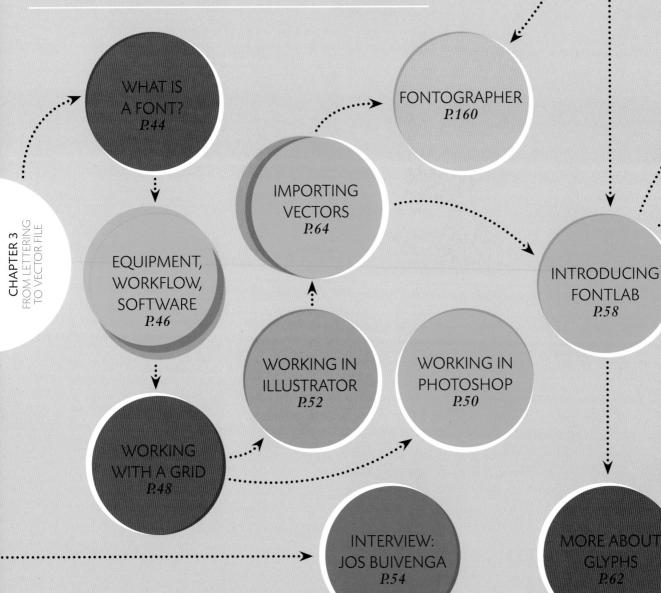

WHAT IS
A FONT?
P.44

FONTOGRAPHER
P.160

CHAPTER 3
FROM LETTERING
TO VECTOR FILE

EQUIPMENT,
WORKFLOW,
SOFTWARE
P.46

IMPORTING
VECTORS
P.64

INTRODUCING
FONTLAB
P.58

WORKING IN
ILLUSTRATOR
P.52

WORKING IN
PHOTOSHOP
P.50

WORKING
WITH A GRID
P.48

INTERVIEW:
JOS BUIVENGA
P.54

MORE ABOUT
GLYPHS
P.62

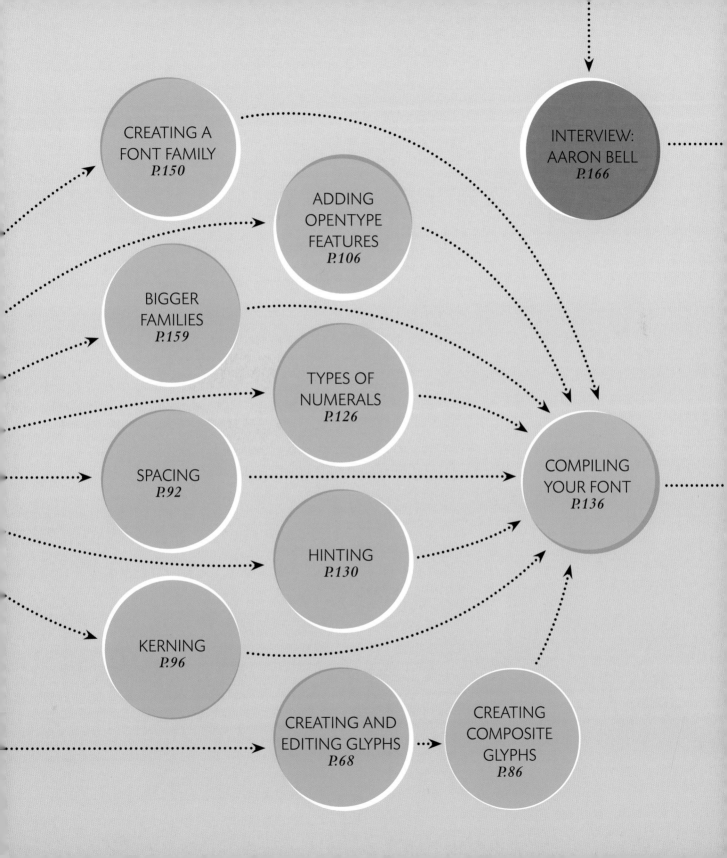

What is a font?

In olden days, printed matter was made via handcrafted chunks of metal glyphs that were set into words, sentences, paragraphs, and pages and then inked and pressed against a blank sheet of paper (image 1).

Traditionally speaking, a font used to be considered a set of cohesively shaped glyphs all at one size. So, for instance, a set of metal glyphs (A—Z, a—z, numerals, punctuation, etc.) of the Garamond family at 12 point would constitute one font. The same family at 14 point would be another font. The same family italicized at 14 point would be another font, as would that family bolded at 14 point.

Today, of course, given that computer fonts can be scaled digitally, we don't need a separate set of glyphs for each point size, and so Garamond is a font that contains cohesive glyphs that scale to any point size. Garamond bold is another font in the same family as Garamond; similarly with Garamond italic, and Garamond bold italic.

The fact that fonts can be digitally scaled is thanks to the magic of vectors. Computer screens are raster devices, composed of a grid of small dots (pixels). If you design a graphic in a raster program (like Photoshop), and you scale it up in size, you lose resolution—the graphic becomes blurrier the bigger you scale it up.

The graphic in image 2 looks great at screen resolution (72dpi), or when significantly shrunk in print, but when pressed into service in print at full size and at 300dpi it begins to degrade into blurriness.

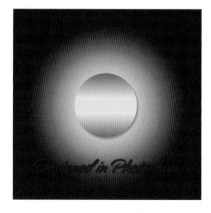

A vector graphic is really less of a graphic and more of a set of instructions. Each part of a vector graphic is composed of primitive geometric shapes that can each be described mathematically. So when a vector graphic is output on a screen (or a page, or any other device), it can be scaled to the appropriate size without any degradation of quality.

The shape in image 3 is composed of vectors, so it can be scaled up or down to any size, with perfect mathematical precision and without any loss of quality.

Fonts are composed of vectors, and this is why you don't need a separate font for each point size—fonts scale with mathematical precision to any size. When we start working with FontLab in Chapter 4, we'll see firsthand how to work with vector editing software. If you work with Adobe Illustrator, you have already been exposed to the world of vector graphics. FontLab's tools are similar to Illustrator's, but are particularly well-suited to working with font shapes.

It's also important to keep in mind that a computer font is actually a piece of software. There are a range of instructions embedded in every font, used by operating systems and layout programs. In Chapter 4 we'll see how to manipulate some of these instructions.

FONT FORMATS

Fonts come in three major software formats: Type 1 Postscript, TrueType, and OpenType. The Type 1 format was developed by Adobe in order to communicate smoothly with Postscript printers. It was long the case that Windows computers had trouble dealing with Type 1 fonts, but the last several versions of Windows have had native support for Type 1. The TrueType font format was developed by Apple and then licensed to Microsoft. It is probably the most ubiquitous font format out there at the moment.

OpenType was developed jointly by Microsoft and Adobe, and is the latest and greatest format. OpenType fonts can contain more glyphs, support more languages, and can embed professional typographic features such as small caps and ligatures. It used to be the case that you'd buy one, say, TrueType font for the basic glyphs, and then another font for small caps, and you'd have to switch between the two fonts in your page layout software in order to get the features you needed in any location in your document. With a fully loaded OpenType font (and an OpenType-aware layout program), you can install one font to get both your basic glyphs and your small caps, along with a host of other features.

Equipment, workflow, and software

Of course, of the many tools you'll use to create your fonts, the most essential is your font design software.

FONTLAB

The most popular, influential program out there right now is FontLab Studio ("FontLab," for short, from here on). FontLab 5—available for both Mac and Windows—is the current version, as of the time of writing, and indeed FontLab has been stuck on version 5 since at least 2006, so that technical details provided here will probably be relevant for quite some time. (FontLab developer Adam Twardoch wrote on the Typophile.org forums of the upcoming 5.5 release: "the 5.5 version number primarily should indicate that the users of current FontLab Studio 5 will feel instantly at home with the new version. There won't be any radical changes, but some important and useful new features, bugfixes, and Mac OS X Intel compatibility." I've heard grumblings that version 6 is quite a ways off in the future.)

COMPETITORS TO FONTLAB

Fontographer—a long-standing competitor to FontLab, which sat dormant for many years until FontLab (the company) acquired the software and released an updated version not too long ago. It's available at fontlab.com for both Windows and Mac. Some font developers swear by the drawing tools available in Fontographer, but the program lacks many of the professional development features of FontLab.

FontForge—a free and open-source program, available at fontforge.sourceforge.net for Linux. (It can also run on Mac operating systems and Windows, but is not a simple installation by any means. For Windows, you have to install a huge chunk of software that essentially emulates Linux; for Macs you have to compile FontForge from source code.) I have heard stories of brave souls who have created fonts with FontForge, but I myself have only a passing familiarity with the program. For fans of open-source software, the appeal of FontForge is obvious; but there are also practical downsides to relying on a small, unpaid community to keep on top of development, bug fixes, and support, and keeping abreast of technological progress. However, if you're a programmer yourself, you can tweak the code to your own satisfaction.

DTL FontMaster—a huge suite of tools, available at fonttools.org. This massive suite comes with a fairly massive price tag as well, so be sure you know what you're getting yourself into before going down the DTL rabbit hole. FontMaster tools are all Windows-based.

RoboFont—a newcomer to the realm of font-creation toolkits. Available only for Mac, at robofont.com, RoboFont was released to a relatively huge amount of buzz in the font design community. Designers are very excited about the possibilities RoboFont brings to the table. The software works with UFO files—an open-source, XML-based font file format that several other font programs utilize. The dream of RoboFont fans is to have a completely UFO-based workflow for font creation, bypassing FontLab's proprietary file format.

Glyphs—another new program, available for Mac at glyphsapp.com. Released at about the same time as RoboFont, Glyphs also came out to a nice bit of fanfare. I think font designers had been waiting so long for FontLab to release something new and exciting, that any glimmer of newness was most welcome.

Regardless of the next big thing, the main piece of font-creation software out there right now is FontLab 5, and FontLab 5 is where we'll spend most of our time in the rest of this book.

OTHER EQUIPMENT

Other equipment and software you'll need will vary depending on the workflow you choose for your font creating. There are several paths to creating a font.

Method 1: Draw your glyphs directly in FontLab—
In terms of workflow, the simplest route is to fire up FontLab or Fontographer and start drawing letters in those programs. In this case, all you need is your font-creation software of choice, and a good mouse or tablet. We'll be spending some quality time with FontLab's excellent vector drawing tools in the "Creating and Editing Glyphs" section of Chapter 4.

Tools you'll need:

- FontLab
- a good mouse
- a steady hand

Method 2: Draw your glyphs on paper—The simplest way to actually design letterforms is to take pen to paper and just draw them by hand, but this leaves you in the unenviable position of getting those drawings into your font-creation software. I'll explain why this is an issue in short order, and walk you through a process for taking drawings and getting them into FontLab.

Tools you'll need:

- a good pen
- good paper
- ruler
- scanner
- Adobe Photoshop (or similar image-editing software)
- ScanFont (optional)
- FontLab

Method 3: Draw your glyphs in Illustrator—Many font creators are used to Adobe Illustrator's tools, and thus draw their letterforms in Illustrator. This gives you digital vectors, which is good, but there is still a workflow issue getting these vectors into your font-creation software. Thankfully, with a little bit of math and some careful preparation, getting your Illustrator vectors into FontLab isn't a huge ordeal.

Tools you'll need:

- a good mouse or Wacom tablet (optional)
- Adobe Illustrator
- FontLab

Working with a grid

As you're drawing your glyphs, whether on paper or in software, it's important to keep to a grid of important measurements. Take a moment to review the vertical metrics (measurements of height) introduced on page 24.

Your glyphs (depending, of course, on design) will share a common baseline, ascender, descender, x-height, and cap height (image 1).

bdfhijkl   ascender

gjpqy

descender

ABCDEFGHIJKLMNOPQRSTUVWXYZabcdefghijklmnopqrstuvwxyz

baseline

ABCDEFGHIJKLMNOPQRSTUVWXYZ   cap height

abcdefghijklmnopqrstuvwxyz   x-height

After you draw your first glyph (there are debates about which letter is the best one to start with; I say start with whatever gets your creative juices flowing), you can start working on a grid that will guide subsequent glyphs. For instance, if you start with an "A," as in image 2, you'll immediately be able to draw your baseline and cap-height lines. If your next glyph is a "p," you'll know where the bottom of its lobe sits (on the baseline), and you'll be able to draw your x-height and descender lines. If next up is your "h," you'll know where its feet sit (on the baseline) and where its arch rises to (the x-height), and when you're done drawing it, you'll be able to draw your ascender line. At this point, you'll have a grid in place that guides subsequent glyphs that you draw in the font. As you draw each glyph in your font, take note of the vertical metrics you're creating as you go. For most fonts, your vertical metrics will be shared among all of your glyphs.

Of course, not all fonts obey a strict grid. Many sans serif fonts, for instance, do not have an ascender line separate from the cap-height line—their tall lowercase letters reach up exactly to the cap height instead of going higher. Many handwriting fonts are the same way—their cap heights are the same as their ascenders—and some handwriting fonts break the grid in all sorts of other interesting and slightly random ways as well. Still, it's a very good idea to draw your glyphs with an explicit grid in place. Then, even if you deviate from it, you'll know exactly what you're deviating from.

If you're drawing your glyphs directly in FontLab, there are ready-made gridlines already provided for you in default positions showing lines for the baseline, x-height, and ascender (image 3). You can change these, and we'll see how in Chapter 4.

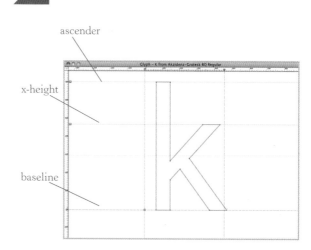

Working in Photoshop

If you're working with hand-drawn lettering, then you're probably going to want to bring those letters into Photoshop for retouching and preparation for importing into FontLab. Unfortunately, FontLab itself cannot handle importing bitmap images. So you have three choices here.

You can use a separate program from FontLab called ScanFont, which specializes in this conversion process. Having used ScanFont in the past, I can certainly recommend it, though of course it would be an added expense in your font-creation arsenal. If you're doing a lot of handwriting fonts however, it might well be worth it.

The second option is to place your scanned images into Illustrator, and use AutoTrace to convert them into vectors.

And your third option is to use Fontographer, which can handle direct importing and tracing of bitmap images.

Also, there's something of a fourth choice: use a Wacom tablet to draw your glyphs directly into Illustrator, in which case no Photoshop would be needed. Unless you're a very experienced Wacom and Illustrator user, this technique won't likely give you as authentic a set of handwritten glyphs as pen and paper would.

SCANNING AND RETOUCHING

Before worrying about vectorizing your drawings, let's talk about scanning and retouching.

The first things to consider in Photoshop, once you've scanned in your drawings, are the contrast and brightness. You might have to increase both the contrast and brightness, depending on your scanner's settings. The goal is to get the most contrast between the paper and ink without losing definition or changing your letters' details. Increasing the brightness will turn the paper whiter; but if you turn things too bright, your letters will start to fade and lose definition.

Increasing the contrast will turn your ink blacker; but if you increase the contrast too much, there's the possibility that the edges of your letter will become unnaturally stark. With my scanner, I find that if I increase the contrast a lot and the brightness just a bit, that gives me a good result, but your mileage may vary.

The scanned glyphs in image 1 show (from top to bottom) before tweaking, after tweaking with too much added brightness, after tweaking with too much contrast, and after tweaking with just the right amount.

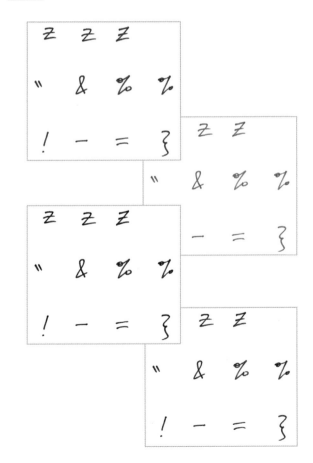

The next thing that may strike you about what you've scanned is that your letters may be all slightly different sizes. Hopefully you've drawn your fonts using a grid! But if you haven't, or you haven't been extremely careful, you'll get some letters that are smaller or larger than others. You'll notice that in image 2, I was not at all careful to draw with a grid—my letters are (not horribly, but definitely) differently sized, and placed on different baselines. This, I am sad to say, came back to cause me troubles in a later stage of the font development process. All of which is to say: draw with a grid whenever you can. (Of course, the downside of a grid for handwriting fonts is that using one might constrict your hand movements unnaturally. Don't sacrifice your handwriting for the sake of perfectly proportioned letters. But know that it will come back to haunt you in the long run if you don't use a grid.)

If you do scan in letters that are differently sized, don't resize your glyphs in Photoshop. Scan in your drawings, tweak them at whatever size they are in Photoshop, and then wait until you have them vectorized to resize them so that they're all at the same scale on the same grid. Resizing bitmap images in Photoshop can make your images lose detail, or change their shapes in unexpected ways.

CONVERTING TO VECTORS

Before you convert your bitmaps to vectors, make sure to do the following:

- Get rid of artifacts, such as dirt and stray pen marks.
- Fill in holes, unless you're going for a grunge look.
- Clean up edges, again, unless you're going for a grunge look.

You can zoom in to your files to make this clean-up process easier, as in images 3 and 4.

If you're bringing your images into ScanFont, save them as true bitmaps—black and white, no shades of gray. Make sure that you're saving a separate copy, because you'll want to keep your non-bitmap versions just in case you ever need to go back to them.

If you're bringing these bitmaps into Illustrator for AutoTracing, experiment with Illustrator's AutoTrace settings. AutoTrace is a wonderful tool, but it wasn't created to handle this process specifically. Make sure your settings are Black and White, and that the box is checked for Ignore White.

Working in Illustrator

Chances are, if you talk to font designers, they will be experts in not only FontLab but Illustrator as well. In fact, some font designers even do much of their glyph design work in Illustrator and then import the results into FontLab for tweaking and font generation. It's no coincidence that font designers like Illustrator—it is a vector-editing tool just like FontLab, and there are a lot of similarities between the two programs.

If you're one of those who likes to draw letters directly in Illustrator, there's really no excuse not to set up a grid! First, make sure that rulers are showing in Illustrator. If you don't see them, go to the View menu and select Show Rulers. Once rulers are showing, you can drag and drop guides onto your Illustrator drawing. Say you've drawn a lowercase "h" (image 1). Now you can drag guides down from the top ruler to the baseline, the x-height, and the ascender. To do this, click anywhere in the top ruler bar, hold the button down, and drag your newly created guide. Dragging guides from the top ruler bar creates horizontal guides; dragging from the left ruler bar creates vertical guides.

The next letter you draw now has helpful guides to constrain it. You can add new guides as applicable. The "g" in image 2 sits on the same baseline I'd already drawn, and reaches up to the same x-height; now I can place a new guide for the descender. Any future glyphs I draw with descenders will reach down to the same line.

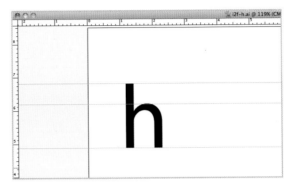

CHANGING SHAPES BY CHANGING BRUSHES

One of the fun and useful things about Illustrator is that you can draw a shape once, and have nearly infinite variations on that shape simply by changing brushes. Image 3 shows an "S" I drew with the default Illustrator paintbrush, followed by five variations using the same stroke but with different brushes.

If you've never changed brushes in Illustrator, it's easy. Just select the shape in question and click in the brush selection box (which may look slightly different depending on the version of Illustrator being used, and the configuration of toolbars selected). A list of default brushes will be available to choose from, as you can see in image 4.

If there aren't enough brushes there to make life interesting, you can open up a different brush library (if you have some installed) by clicking on the tiny arrow in the upper right of the brush selection box, and following the fly-out menus (image 5).

Additional brushes are also easy to find on the web, and easy to install in Illustrator. Check the Illustrator documentation for instructions on how to install brushes. Be a little careful of the brushes you install—download brushes only from sources you trust, since it's not impossible that a bad brush could give Illustrator hiccups.

FROM ILLUSTRATOR TO FONTLAB

Illustrator is a vector drawing tool, and, thankfully FontLab speaks the same vector language as Illustrator. You can take a set of vectors in Illustrator, copy them, and paste them directly into FontLab.

One problem with this scenario is sizing. The odds are next to nil that a glyph you draw in Illustrator will scale to the appropriate size in FontLab, as you can see with this "A" in image 6.

I'll cover how to import Illustrator vectors into FontLab at the proper scale on page 64.

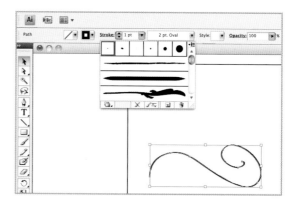

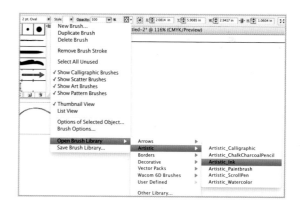

Jos Buivenga

Jos Buivenga can be passionate about a lot of things. He loves to paint and listen to music, but nothing challenges and rewards him more than designing type. He is the founder of exljbris, the one-man Dutch font foundry through which he releases and offers his typefaces.

For fifteen years, his online friends and fans could follow the development of his typefaces and download the results at no cost. In 2008, while still working as an art director at an advertising agency, he released his first commercial typeface, Museo, with several weights offered free of charge.

That strategy paid off, and Museo became a huge bestseller. Partly thanks to that success, Buivenga now calls himself a full-time type designer.

Do you remember the moment you decided you wanted to actually create a font? Looking back, once you started your first font, do you think you were well prepared for the undertaking?

"That moment was long ago somewhere in 1994 when I was playing around with my first Mac and thought that it would be great if I could type a letterset in my own font. I was utterly unprepared. I liked that because I love to find things out myself."

"There's always room for good type."

Any lessons learned from font creation that you'd share with a beginner?

"I learned that it is very important for me to spend humongous amounts of times just looking at the screen or at prints on the wall to get the best grip on every aspect of my current typeface design."

"I saw my first font, Delicious, used in a whole page newspaper ad. That was pretty exciting."

Font creation can be a very solitary endeavor. Do you feel like it's important to connect with other font designers? What sorts of outlets are important along these lines? Social media? Conferences?

"It's always good to have connections with other type designers so you can share knowledge and experience. Social media, conferences, and advertising are very important if you want to market your fonts. You can make the most beautiful stuff, but if people don't know that it's there you won't sell a single font."

What is your font creation process?
Do you start with pencil and paper?
Do you draw glyphs directly in software?
Do you have an idea before you start
drawing glyphs, or do you sit down and
see what happens? What software do you
use to create fonts?

"I don't have a standard way of starting a design. It can start with an idea or a sketch. Eventually I always end up drawing it in FontLab. The software I use includes FontLab, Superpolator, Prepolator, and Glyphs. Besides that, I also use the iKern service of Igino Marini."

Do you remember the first time
you saw a font of yours used on
product packaging or a website?

"I saw my first font, Delicious, used in a whole page newspaper ad. That was pretty exciting."

What are some of your favorite
fonts by other designers?

"There were three typefaces I found really special when I was discovering how to make my own type about 15 years ago: FF Scala, FF Balance, and FF Quadraat."

"You can make the most beautiful stuff, but if people don't know that it's there you won't sell a single font. "

Do you ever go back and revise your
fonts once they've been published?

"I don't revise my fonts unless there's a need to correct something that's not looking or working right."

Can the industry support the increasing
number of designers and font releases
coming out?

"There's always room for good type."

Jos Buivenga

1.

2.

Gravlax

From '*trench*' & lax '*salmon*' (fish)

Calluna

Is also the name of a so-called heather plant.

HAMSTRING

A (QUADRUPED'S) HOCK!

luckiést

Q&A: 32 questions should be answered

Gravlax

From '*trench*' & lax '*salmon*' (fish)

Calluna

Is also the name of a so-called heather plant.

HAMSTRING

A (QUADRUPED'S) HOCK!

luckiést

Q&A: 32 questions should be answered

3.

museo
museo
museo
museo
museo

100 300 **500** **700** **900**

4.

SAN FRANCISCO
heavy
World Tournament 2011
MOTELS
Water Flow (4,365.80 Kgs/m^2)
Wolga Sturgeon
Astrakan

1. Calluna: prints and reads beautifully in large tracts of text.

2. Calluna Sans: a humanist sans serif based on the Calluna family.

3. Museo: the uppercase "U" came to Jos "like an image in a daydream."

4. Museo Sans Rounded: created as a complement to Museo.

5. Geotica: built from simple geometrical line elements to form something grand.

Machina
for only £4,00?
WOW

5.

Astonished
ZELHEM
Best of Luck
Add Céruleum & be

Chapter 4

FONT CREATION SOFTWARE TUTORIALS

Introducing FontLab

FontLab is essentially a vector editing program, with font creation capabilities. It's the program in which most font creators spend the bulk of their time. In the next few sections, we'll be taking a close look at some of FontLab's capabilities and quirks.

✳ ✳ ✳ *FontLab Tutorial*

WORKING IN FONTLAB

Get ready to dive into the software in which you'll be spending many precious hours of the next stage of your life! (Don't worry—it's completely worth it.) Let's fire it up, create a new font file, and explore FontLab's interface.

1.

When you start FontLab and create a new font file (File menu > New), you're presented with a matrix of empty glyph boxes, in what we'll call the "main window" (see image below).

This is the default set of glyphs that FontLab decides you'll need in order to have a workable font. It's definitely a big enough list to get you started, but you're not stuck with this set of glyphs— you can add more glyphs to your font at any time, by going to the Glyph menu and selecting Generate Glyphs. (Note that you don't have to create all of the glyphs that FontLab suggests you need. I once created a custom font for a client with only three glyphs in it, one of which was a space!)

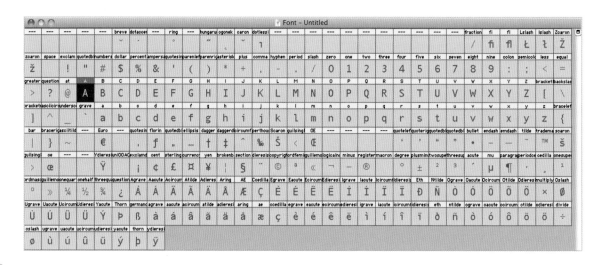

2.

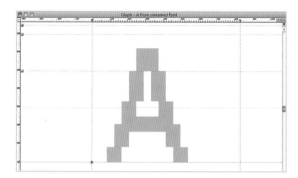

FontLab conveniently puts a light gray background image of a generic letter in each glyph cell, in case you are confused about which character you're working with. If you double-click on a glyph cell, you'll create a separate glyph-editing window with that gray background image enlarged within it.

3.

You can leave this background image there if you like, but I find it very distracting, and when I start designing a glyph in the glyph-editing window, the first thing I generally do is go to the View menu, and choose Show Layers/Background. This toggles on and off the background gray letters in the glyph-editing window. (Note that this choice will only be available while you have a glyph-editing window open. Also note that you can, instead of hiding the background layer, delete each background image one at a time, by double clicking anywhere in the vicinity of the background image—this should highlight the background, and you can simply press the Delete key to get rid of it.)

4.

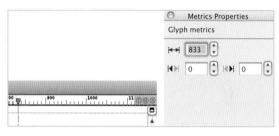

The first things you'll see in the glyph-editing window are horizontal and vertical lines. The two vertical dashed lines represent the glyph's sidebearings. FontLab puts these sidebearings at a reasonable default location, but you'll be changing these in short order. You can manipulate sidebearings by simply clicking on them and dragging them horizontally. You can also fine-tune their positions by right-clicking on a sidebearing and selecting "properties" from the pop-up menu.

5.

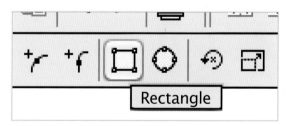

Let's create a shape to put into our glyph-editing window, so that we can see better how sidebearings work. Click on the button with the rectangle icon on it near the top of the screen.

Continues...

59

6.

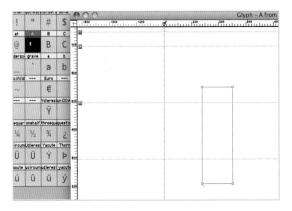

Now click your cursor somewhere in the middle of the glyph-editing window and drag it slowly outward and down.

7

With the sidebearings at their default positions, if you've drawn a skinny enough box, there will be too much room around your makeshift "A." If you were to create a font with this glyph, install it on your system, and then use it to print out a version of itself, you'd see that the sidebearings are not set well here. A glyph with too distant sidebearings creates too much space in between letters when you use the font in any other program.

8

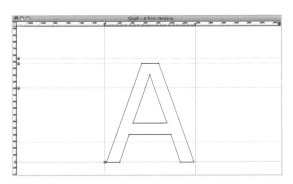

Now let's go ahead and double click on the "A" cell. This opens up a separate window in which you could edit the "A" glyph if you so desired. Let's take a look at some of the features of this glyph-editing window. Notice that the sidebearings are readily apparent, as are some of the important vertical metrics we've been talking about: baseline, x-height, cap height, ascender, and descender. If you can't see all of the vertical metrics lines, you can zoom out of the glyph to see more, simply by clicking in the box in the lower left where it displays a percent value.

9

You can change the right sidebearing by grabbing it and dragging it either left or right. (It's rare that I change the left sidebearing—I find it more intuitive to keep it fixed, and move the entire glyph left or right to change its proximity to the left sidebearing.) You might think that the vertical metric lines are similarly draggable, but they're not. Since those measures are not specific to any one glyph, but rather are applicable to the entire font, you'll specify (and/or have FontLab calculate automatically) them in the "Font Info" window, after all of your glyphs are created.

A NOTE ABOUT UNICODE

Unicode is a standard that was developed to represent (or encode) letters of alphabets so that they can be transmitted and decoded by computers.

You can open any installed font on your system with FontLab. Go to File/Open Installed and select any font you like. (Verdana is a good one to open, if you have it installed. That's what I used in the images below.) You'll notice that by default the matrix of glyphs displayed in the main window is labeled in yellow with odd-looking combinations of numbers and letters (image 1). These are the Unicode character names of the glyphs.

You can change these labels in FontLab's main window to something more user-friendly by clicking on the pull-down list at the bottom of the screen and choosing "Name." Now you can see that "A" is "A," rather than "0041" (image 2).

More about glyphs

It's one of the great disservices of the American education system that we are taught that there are 26 letters in the English alphabet. Even as elementary-school teachers are showing us the difference between uppercase and lowercase letters, they still stick to their story that there are only 26 letters. Even as they show us how to use punctuation and quotation marks, it's all just about those 26 letters.

Fast forward to today. You are an aspiring font creator, and you fire up FontLab for the first time; 229 empty boxes stare out at you, waiting to be filled with vectory goodness. You curse the day your teachers taught you that there are only 26 letters in the Latin alphabet.

So, yes, there are 26 lowercase letters for you to turn into glyphs. There are also 26 uppercase. There are punctuation marks, quotation marks, currency symbols, ampersands, mathematical symbols, dashes, fractions, parentheses, braces, brackets, numerals, and many more glyphs to be created. Even the lowly space character needs some design—you'll be setting up sidebearings for it, in order to tell software that uses your font how much horizontal room to provide when someone types a space. On top of everything else, there are accents and accented characters to deal with.

If you're like me, you might have thought that fonts have letter glyphs, such as "e," and accent glyphs, such as "´" (the acute), and that if you need an "é" in your document, your word-processing software would take the "e" and the acute, and compose them together on the fly. There is some validity to this scenario, in that some software can manage the composition of accented characters out of two (or more) glyphs—and, indeed, even the Unicode encoding standard was built with this possibility in mind. But there's no piece of software that can compose an accented glyph as well as a skilled font designer. There's a lot of artistry that goes into the placement of accents on a letter, and the acute can vary in both size and angle from one accented character to the next. And so, when you are creating a font in FontLab, you will be creating not just the standard alphabet glyphs, and not just accent glyphs—you will also be composing accented characters. If you're smart, you'll be composing a whole lot of them—not just the ones FontLab suggests you create.

I've had emails from people thanking me for including specific (and obscure) glyphs in some of my fonts. Never underestimate the importance of even the most obscure glyphs. Someone out there will be very thankful if you include them in your fonts.

NON-LATIN GLYPHS

There are Greek, Cyrillic, Arabic, Hebrew, Chinese, Japanese, and Korean glyphs to be created, if you're up for the challenge. It's rather rare for a Latin font to have a full complement of even one of these languages along with its Latin glyphs, but it's not unheard of. Before you start creating glyphs from other languages, be sure you really know what these languages look like and how they work. Study unfamiliar glyphs extensively before trying to create them and ask for feedback from language experts. Before releasing my open-source font Lavoisier, I enlisted the help of Sergiy Tkachenko to fill out the font's complement of Cyrillic glyphs. I knew next to nothing about Cyrillic at the time, and Sergiy was an expert who created a huge number of glyphs for me.

FINE POINTS

The letter J

The "J" is an interesting glyph, with a huge variety of implementations across fonts. Image 1 shows a variety of "J" glyphs from various fonts. The top row of type depicts a number of sans serif fonts with each "J" resting snugly on the baseline, and varying drawings of the tops of the glyph. From left to right, the fonts are Myriad Pro, Helvetica, Verdana, and Logo Sans. The second row also sits each "J" on the baseline, but all are serif fonts. Note the varying drawings of the terminals of each "J." From left to right, these fonts are Clarendon Text, American Typewriter, Basilia and Museo. The final row shows two serif and two sans serif fonts, each with a "J" that descends below the baseline. From left to right, the fonts are Weiss BT, Winthorpe, Gibson and Montag.

If you're undecided on how to treat the "J" in a font you're developing, try creating one "J" that you think might work best in most situations, and then create alternate "J" glyphs using OpenType features, as detailed on page 106.

Importing vectors

✳ ✳ ✳ *FontLab Tutorial*

ILLUSTRATOR AND FONTLAB

Here's how to get your hard work from Illustrator into FontLab. Assuming that you've already drawn your letterforms in Illustrator, the next step is to measure your drawings, along with all of the important vertical metric measures: baseline, descender, x-height, caps height, and ascender. Make sure your rulers are showing in Illustrator (ctrl-R), and drag some guides from the top ruler to all of the key heights of your forms.

In this illustration, I'm using millimeters as my units, but you can use whatever you're comfortable with.

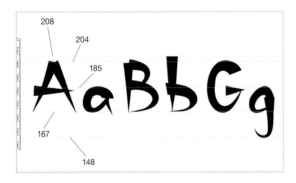

1

em square	cap height	x height	ascender	descender
208	204	185	208	148
− 148	− 167	− 167	− 167	− 167
60	37	18	41	**−19**

Note the position of each of your guides, and write them down, as you'll be doing some math with them in short order. FontLab measures its fonts in terms of UPM, or "Units Per eM," and so we have to find a way to go from whatever units you're using in Illustrator to UPM. The first step is to measure the "em square" (the height from the descender to the ascender of your typeface) in Illustrator. The em square of this example is 60 millimeters, since the distance from the ascender (at 208) to the descender (at 148) is 60.

2

$$\underline{\text{UPM} = 1000} \quad \rightarrow \quad 1000 \text{ units per em}$$

(37 / 60) x 1000 =	**617**	**cap height**
(18 / 60) x 1000 =	**300**	**x height**
(41 / 60) x 1000 =	**683**	**ascender**
(− 19 / 60) x 1000 =	**− 317**	**descender**

While we're at it, let's measure the rest of the vertical metrics in our Illustrator units. The standard UPM size in FontLab is 1,000, so let's use that in our further calculations.

3

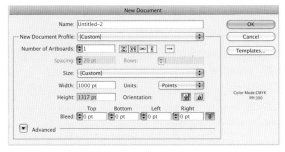

These numbers are going to be the heights of our guides for a new Illustrator document that we will use for copying and pasting glyphs from Illustrator to FontLab. So let's create a new Illustrator document, in points, with the height of 1,000 + the length of your descender: in this case, 1,000 + 317 = 1,317.

4

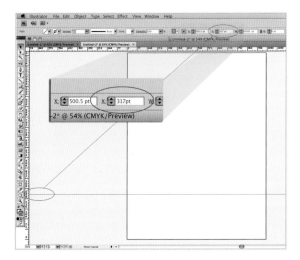

Next, we have to put our guides into place. Make sure your guides are not locked, then drag a vertical guide to somewhere near the value of your descender length. Select your guide, then click on the "transform" link to set the exact value.

5

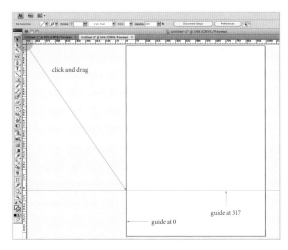

Once that guide is set, place a horizontal guide at zero. Then click on the upper-left corner where the two rulers intersect, and drag to the intersection of zero and (in this case) 317. This sets your zero point for your rulers.

6

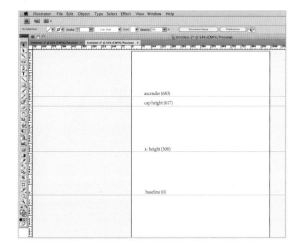

Now you can place more guides, according to the numbers for ascender, caps height, and x-height that you calculated in step 2.

Continues…

7

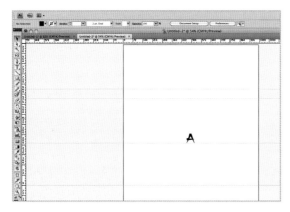

Go back to your Illustrator document in which your new typeface drawings reside. Select your "A" and copy it. Then switch back to your new guideline document and paste the "A" into it.

8

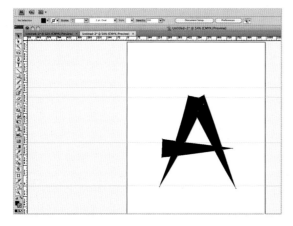

It's the wrong size, but this is easy to remedy, thanks to our handy guides. Click on the form, hold down the shift key (to make sure you resize the shape proportionately), and resize so that the shape conforms to your guides.

9

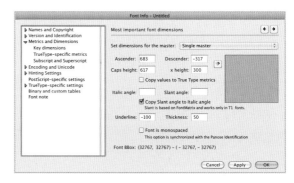

Now we need a new FontLab file. Go ahead and create one, and then go to the File menu, select "Font Info," expand the "Metrics and Dimensions" node, and click on the "Key Dimensions" option. Set the Ascender, Descender, Caps Height, and X-Height values to (in this case) 683, -317, 617, and 300.

10

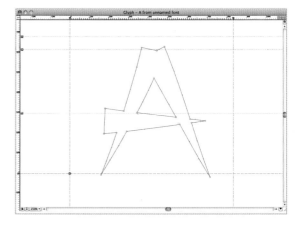

Go back to Illustrator, select your newly sized "A", and copy it. Then go back to FontLab, open up your "A" glyph window, and paste. You now have a perfectly sized glyph.

FINE POINTS
T–heights

Image 1 shows Minion Pro's basic alphabet. If you consider the usual top three vertical metrics—ascender, cap height, and x-height—there's one glyph that sticks out like a proverbial sore thumb: the lowercase "t." The apex of the "t" reaches above the x-height, but sits below the cap height.

I have found no accepted terminology for the measure of the top of the "t," and propose that we give an obvious name to this singular vertical metric: t-height.

The "t" of a typical serif font has a crossbar that sits at the font's x-height, and a t-height somewhere between the x-height and the cap height. Typical sans serif fonts adhere to the same basic rule, but geometric sans serif fonts and handwriting fonts often deviate from this rule, with their t-heights being close to their cap heights. Image 2 shows the t-heights of various fonts; in the left-hand column from top to bottom is Adobe Garamond Pro, Helvetica, Toronto Subway, and Scrap Casual. In the right-hand column from top to bottom is Baskerville, Square 721, Century Gothic, and AJHand.

AaBbCcDdEeFfGgHhIi
JjKkLlMmNnOoPpQq
RrSsTtUuVvWwXxYyZz

Ehct

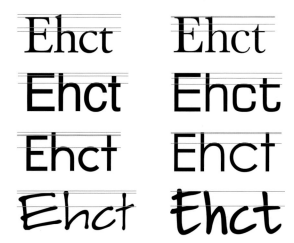

Creating and editing glyphs

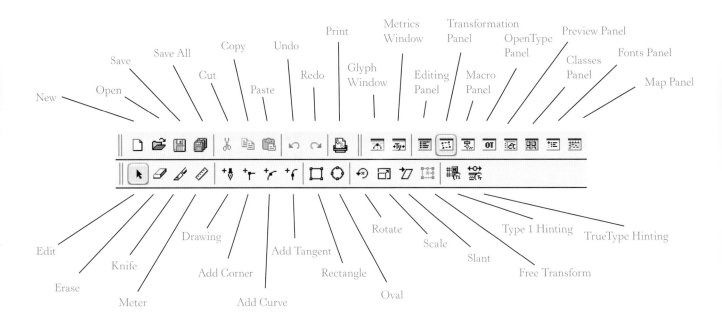

New · Open · Save · Save All · Cut · Copy · Paste · Undo · Redo · Print · Glyph Window · Metrics Window · Editing Panel · Transformation Panel · Macro Panel · OpenType Panel · Preview Panel · Classes Panel · Fonts Panel · Map Panel

Edit · Erase · Knife · Meter · Drawing · Add Corner · Add Curve · Add Tangent · Rectangle · Oval · Rotate · Scale · Slant · Free Transform · Type 1 Hinting · TrueType Hinting

Above is an annotated screenshot of the toolbars I have displayed whenever I'm working in FontLab. To show or hide toolbars, go to the View menu, and choose Toolbars. I have these toggled on at all times: Standard, Panels, and Tools.

SHAPES IN FONTLAB

You'll notice that in the main window your rectangle appears as a solid box, while in the editor window it appears as just an outline. In fact, in FontLab straight lines and curves (just as in geometry) have no intrinsic width at all. If you were to draw a straight line in a FontLab glyph, nothing would display in the font itself. If you want a very thin line in one of your glyphs, you have to draw a very skinny rectangle. In other words, an area has to be bounded by curves in order for FontLab to be able to translate that into a displayable shape in your font.

✳✳✳ *FontLab Tutorial*
WORKING WITH RECTANGLES

FontLab provides you with several primitive shapes to get you started drawing glyphs. Let's dive right in with the rectangle tool.

1

Create a brand-new font file in FontLab. (Click on the "File/New" menu item, or on the New button in the standard toolbar.) When the glyph matrix in the main window is displayed, double-click on the "T" cell to begin creating your capital T glyph. (If you haven't already, and the gray background image of a "T" is showing in your editing window, go to the View/Show Layers/Background menu item, and toggle the background off.)

2

Now click on the rectangle button and move your cursor into the editing area. You'll notice that FontLab's cursor changes to show you precisely where one corner of your rectangle will be as soon as you click your mouse. Move the cursor to the guideline for the cap height and click and drag (while continuing to hold down the mouse button) slowly to the right and down. Release the mouse button when you have drawn what seems to be a suitable top bar for your "T."

3

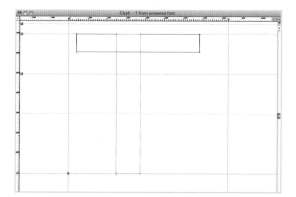

The rectangle tool remains selected after you've created a rectangle. So let's go ahead and complete the stem of our "T" by clicking on the cap-height line and dragging down and to the right, all the way down to the baseline.

Continues...

4

At the time of writing, there's no FontLab tool for centering two shapes with each other, so in order to center the stem with the top bar of your "T" you have two choices: aligning them by eye, or by doing a little bit of arithmetic. The aligning-by-eye method may not be the right choice in this case (you probably want things exactly centered here), but there are plenty of instances in font design where visual balance is much more important than mathematical balance.

6

FontLab works with a coordinate system, with the origin (0, 0) being the point where the left sidebearing meets the baseline. The first number, or x-coordinate, specifies how far to the right or the left of the origin you are; the second number, or y-coordinate, specifies how far up or down from the origin you are.

5

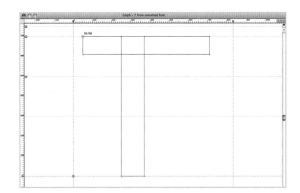

If you want the stem to be perfectly, mathematically centered with your top bar, then follow the next few steps. Click on the top-left node of the top bar. (I'll be using the terms "node" and "point" interchangeably.) It will be outlined in red to show that it's selected, and its coordinates will be shown.

7

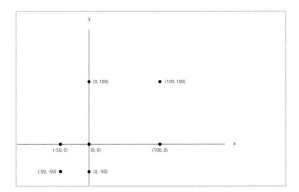

As you go to the right from the origin, the x-coordinate increases, so that if you're, say, 100 units out, you're at (100, 0). As you go up from the origin, the y-coordinate increases, so that when you're, say, 100 units up, you're at (0, 100). If you're 100 units out and up from the origin, you're at (100, 100). You can be at negative coordinates as well. At 50 units down from the origin, and 50 units to the left, you're at (-50, -50).

8

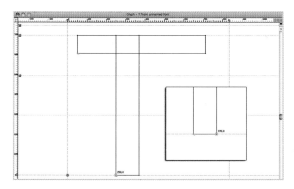

The top-left point of the top bar I drew is at (50, 700). Write down the coordinates of your point, and then select the top-right point of the top bar. Mine is at (710, 700). Write down your coordinates. The width of my top bar is 710 − 50 = 660. Divide that in half and add in the starting position to get the exact center of the top bar: that's 330 + 50 = 380. Now let's measure the width of your stem. Mine goes from 250 to 370.

9

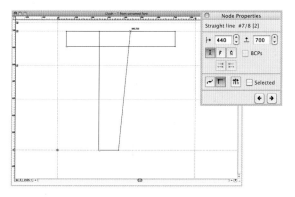

My stem is 120 units wide. Divide that in half to get 60. So the stem of my "T," in order to be centered with the top bar, should straddle the center of the top bar at 380; that is, it should go from 320 (380 − 60) to 440 (380 + 60). Now how do we get it there? Select your top-right stem point and make sure you have the Node Properties window open (Edit/Properties), and type 440 (or whatever number you calculated for yourself) in the horizontal position field. Press Enter to get FontLab to accept your change, and you'll see the point move to its new location.

10

Now do the same for the bottom-right stem point. Move it to 440 (or whatever you calculated) in the horizontal position. Now you have to move the left points of the stem. Use the same procedure to move them to 320 in the horizontal position. Your stem is now centered with your top bar!

There are other ways to move points in FontLab. You can just click on one and drag it anywhere you like. You can also click on a point to select it, and then use the arrow keys on your keyboard to move the point one unit at a time. However, sometimes there is no substitute for mathematical precision when you're moving points, and so you might have to do a little math from time to time.

11

There's one more thing you should know about the rectangle tool. You can use it to draw a perfect square by holding down your Shift key while dragging the tool to size your shape.

✳✱✱ *FontLab Tutorial*

WORKING WITH OVALS

Another primitive tool of great utility is the oval tool.

2

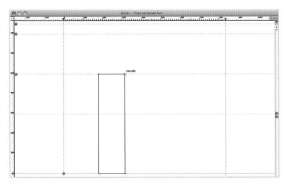

Check to make sure that your points are in the right spots. Click on each upper point and make sure that they're at a height of 500. If not, use either the Properties window or the arrow keys to move them to the default x-height of 500. (You can change this x-height if you want to.) Likewise, check your baseline points to make sure they're actually on the baseline, at a height of 0. I drew my first shape one unit too short. Selecting both top nodes and nudging them up will fix that.

1

Let's create a basic "i" glyph using the rectangle tool and the oval tool. Get back to your main screen, and double-click on the "i" cell to open it up in the editing window. Now select the rectangle tool and create a vertical rectangle extending up from the baseline to the font's x-height.

3

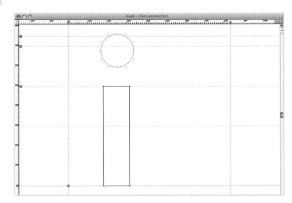

Now select the oval tool and click on the canvas above the rectangle. A good spot is slightly above the ascender line, and slightly to the left of the left side of the rectangle you just drew. While dragging your new oval down and to the right, keep the Shift key pressed to keep it a perfect circle. Release the mouse when the circle is slightly wider than the width of your rectangle.

4

Your circle will not, unless you are either incredibly gifted or incredibly lucky, be in the exact right place. So here's how to move it. Choose the Edit tool from the toolbox, and press ctrl-U to deselect any and all objects that may be selected. Now double-click on a curve of the circle you've just created. (Don't double-click on one of the circle's four points—that will just select the point you've clicked, not the entire circle.) The circle's outline will turn red, indicating that the entire shape is now actively selected. You can now just click on the circle (that is, on the circle's outline, not inside the circle) and drag it wherever you like.

5

We can go through some exacting mathematical detail to ensure that the circle is perfectly aligned with the rectangle's midpoint. Calculate the horizontal midpoint of the rectangle by taking the horizontal position of the bottom-left point, subtracting it from the horizontal position of the bottom-right point, and dividing that number by two; then move the circle until both of the middle points' horizontal positions are at that number. Alternatively, you could align it by eye.

6

A couple of important design considerations crop up at this point as well. Generally speaking, the dot of an "i" is slightly wider than the rectangle below it. Also, generally, if the dot is indeed a circle (some fonts have dots that are rectangular), the top of that circle will be slightly above the ascender line. This harkens back to our earlier discussion of overshoots—generally, curved tops and bottoms sit slightly above and below their straight-lined counterparts, because of an optical phenomenon that makes curved shapes seem as if they don't descend and ascend quite as far as they actually do.

DOTTING THE I

There isn't really a standard for the shape and height of an "i's" dot. Below is a comparison of Myriad Pro Bold (top left), Pluto Medium (top right), Helvetica Bold (bottom left), and Adobe Garamond Pro Bold (bottom right). Myriad has an ascender higher than the cap height, but the dot of its "i" rises slightly above the cap height, not the ascender. Helvetica has a square dot for its "i" and it levels off at the cap height, which is the same as its ascender. Pluto has an ascender height different from its cap height, and the round dot of its "i" tops out above the ascender. Garamond has an ascender higher than its cap height, but its "i's" dot actually sits lower than the cap height. If you study some of your favorite fonts, you'll see that these sorts of quirks abound and give fonts a unique flavor.

✳✱✳ *FontLab Tutorial*
COMBINING SHAPES

Going back to the "T" we created on page 71, go to the main window and double-click on the "T" cell; you'll see the two rectangles we made in the editing window. Many of the glyphs you create will start out as a group of individual shapes. Eventually, you'll want to combine all of these shapes in each of your glyphs so that your font doesn't have to worry about proper intersections and overlapping areas. You don't need those headaches; neither do your font's users. I leave all my glyphs as groups of separate shapes until quite late in the font's development, save a copy of that version of the font, then get to work combining shapes. For this case, let's just combine our T's two rectangles.

2

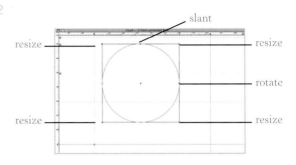

Now let's create an "O." Go back to the main window and double-click on the "O" cell to open it up in the editing window. Select the oval tool, and draw a perfect circle (holding down the Shift key as you drag) that goes from just above the cap-height line to just below the baseline. (This gives us the proper overshoots for our curved glyphs.) If you drew the circle too small or too large, you can either delete it or resize it. To resize it, make sure the whole shape is selected, and then double-click on the circle's outline. This invokes FontLab's transform mode on the shape, signaled by the gray rectangle that surrounds your shape.

1

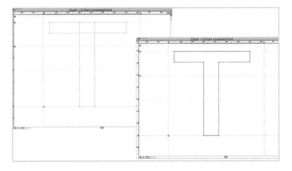

In the font-editing window for the "T," press ctrl-A to select every point and shape in the glyph. The two rectangles will turn red, showing that they are actively selected. Now either press ctrl-F10, or go to the Contour menu and select Transform/Merge Contours. The overlapping rectangles are turned into one conglomerate shape—overlapping areas are merged, resulting in a simpler, more computer-friendly shape (less computationally intensive, and less prone to display problems).

3

You can now resize the circle by dragging on one of the four corners of the transform square (to keep the shape a perfect circle as you resize it, hold down the Shift key as you drag). You could also rotate the circle (of course, rotating a circle still gives you a circle in the exact same position, so it's not a useful tool for this shape) by dragging on the handle on the middle of the right side of the transform square; and you could slant the circle by dragging on the handle on the middle of the top side of the transform square. Feel free to play around with these transform handles now. You can always back out of any action you perform by undoing it with ctrl-Z.

4

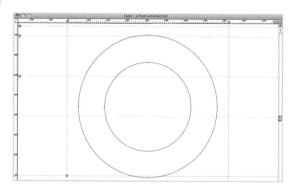

Once your circle is the right size and in the right location, take a look back at the main screen. You'll see that your "O" is now just a filled, black circle. We need a way to knock out the inside of that circle. Go back to the edit window and make a new circle. You have two options here. First, you could just select the oval tool and draw a new circle; second, you could select your old circle, and then press ctrl-C to copy it, and ctrl-V to paste a copy of it onto the canvas. Whichever you choose, make sure your new circle is smaller than your old one.

5

If you check the main window again, you'll see that as far as FontLab is concerned, you haven't accomplished anything with this new circle—it's a black hole on top of a black hole, and so the bigger black hole is unaffected. We need to figure out how to knock out the little hole from the big one.

Let's get precise here and align our two circles perfectly with one another. Click once on the big circle's topmost point. Write down its horizontal coordinate (the first number of the pair of numbers displayed near the point). Now click once on the little circle's topmost point. See how its horizontal coordinate compares to the number you just wrote down. If you lined up the circles by eye carefully, it shouldn't be too far off. If it's greater by a little, then you have to move the little circle over to the left the number of the difference between the two horizontal coordinates. Select the entire little circle and press the left arrow that number of times. The same goes for the case where the little circle's coordinate is less than the big circle's. Select the entire little circle and nudge it to the right that number of times.

6

Now we can do some knocking out. Select both entire circles by pressing ctrl-A. Both circles should be colored red now. Go to the Contour menu, and select Transform/Delete Intersection. This takes the part where both circles overlap and removes it, creating a single shape with a hole in it. If you go back to the main window, you'll see that your "O" now has a beautiful hole in it. Go back to the editing window with the "O" in it. Even though you now have a shape with a hole in it, the inner and outer rings of that shape can still be manipulated separately. So if you don't like the position of the inner hole, you can double-click on it and drag or nudge it around. Go ahead and experiment, and check the results by looking at the main window to get a preview of what your mutated "O" looks like.

You can also select the inner circle (turning it red in the editing window) and then double-click on the selected curve, invoking the transform mode (you'll see a gray rectangle around the selected curve). Transform the curve by resizing it with the corner handles, rotating it with the right-side handle, or slanting it with the top handle.

7

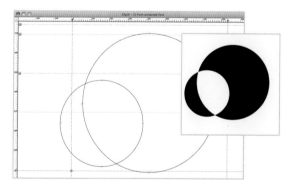

If you drag the inner circle partly outside of the outer circle, you'll see that the hole remains wherever the inner circle is still inside the outer, but that wherever the inner circle ventures outside, it will display as not a hole but as a solid shape. After you've deleted the intersection of the two circles, your glyph behaves as a proper "O" with an empty middle. You can see this dramatically by moving the inner circle partly outside of the outer circle.

✳ ✳ ✱ *FontLab Tutorial*

ABOUT BÉZIER CURVES

Pronounced either "BEH-Zee-Ay" or "BAY-Zee-Ay" depending upon whom you ask, the curves have an intimidating name, but once you get used to working with them in FontLab you'll see that they're pretty easy to use. (Incidentally, Bézier curves are a mainstay of Adobe Illustrator as well. The tools in Illustrator are slightly different, but the principles are the same.)

1

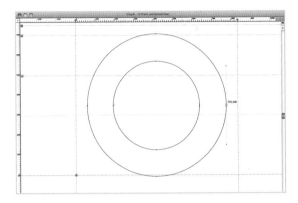

Get back into the editing window for your "O," and click once on the rightmost point of the glyph. Notice that the point, once selected, shows two handles sprouting off of it, in opposite directions from one another. Each node in a shape has two handles extending from it. These handles can be manipulated to change the shape's contour.

2

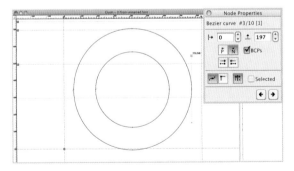

If you click once on either of these handles, FontLab will display its coordinates. You can move these handles just as if you were moving any normal point: click on it and drag it; click on it and use the arrow keys to nudge it in any direction; or type new coordinates into the Properties window. In the Properties window the coordinates for Bezier handles are relative to their parent's coordinates. Here, the handle's coordinates are (0, 197), meaning that they are zero units to the right of the parent point, and 197 units above the parent point.

3

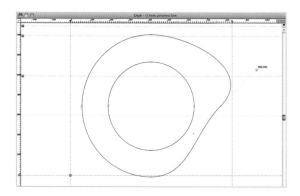

Experiment with dragging around the top handle of the rightmost point you've selected. Notice that its opposite handle remains opposite of it, no matter which way you drag it. Notice also that you can lengthen and shorten it, and that by doing so you change the contour of the "O" in interesting ways.

4

Now double-click on the rightmost point of the "O." If you have the Properties panel open, you may notice that the point has changed from a smooth connection point to a sharp connection point. You can toggle between the two types of points by double-clicking on the point in question, or by selecting the point and then toggling between the smooth and sharp connection buttons in the Properties panel.

5

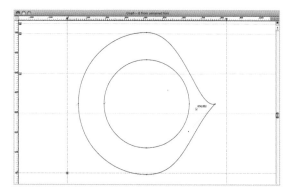

Now click once on the upper handle of the rightmost point, and drag it around. Notice what has happened now that your parent point is a sharp connection instead of a smooth one—the two handles of the point now move independently of one another.

6

Double-click on the parent point to change it back to a smooth connection. Notice that FontLab has once again connected the two handles so that they are opposite one another, and has done so in a way that averages the two handles' directions, i.e., it doesn't arbitrarily pick one of the handles and make that the primary one opposite from which the other handle has to snap. This comes in handy when you're trying to smooth out curves in your glyphs.

✳ ✳ ✱ *FontLab Tutorial*

DRAGGING CURVES INSTEAD OF POINTS/HANDLES

You can also change the shapes of your curves by actually dragging the curves themselves, not the curves' points.

3

If, instead of dragging an unselected curve as you've just been doing, you actually select two adjacent points (thus selecting the curve between those points as well), something different happens when you drag that curve around. You can select two adjacent points by either clicking on one point and then holding the Shift key while you click on the second point, or you could click and drag the mouse over both points and release the mouse when both points have been covered by your mouse movement. (In this second case, be careful to select only the two points you want—it's easy to accidentally grab a stray point that's in the way of your mouse.) In either case, the two points will be highlighted red to show that you've selected them, as will the curve in between those points.

1

Go back to your "O" in the editing window, make sure nothing is selected (you can simply click anywhere off the glyph in the editing window, or press ctrl-U to deselect everything), and click and drag anywhere on the outermost curve of the glyph (without actually selecting a point).

4

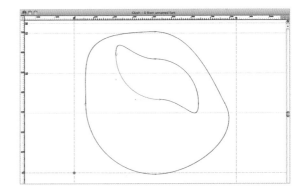

Now click on the selected curve and drag it around. The curve itself will change position as you drag it, but will not change shape. The adjacent curves, however, will change shape as you drag your curve around.

Select another adjacent point (by holding Shift while you click on it), and drag your bigger curve around. Does it behave the way you expect? (You're not constrained to picking adjacent points, by the way. Go ahead and select two non-adjacent points on your "O," and drag them around. Watch how FontLab reacts.)

2

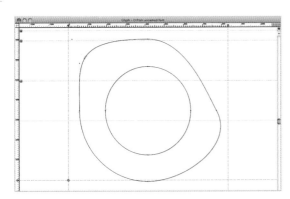

The curve you've selected between the two points will move, while the rest of the curve beyond those two points will remain stationary. Experiment with moving curves like this for a little while, in order to get a feel for how FontLab treats its curves.

ADDING POINTS

Sometimes a curve you've created won't allow you to tweak it in the way you'd like it. It might be the case that you need to add a point or two to the curve so that you have more granularity in what you're grabbing, moving, and changing. Let's try this out on the poor, misshapen "O" in image 1. It's a simple procedure.

First, make sure that no points or curves are already selected (ctrl-U), and that the Edit tool is selected. Now select a point on the curve near where you want the new point to be, click on the drawing tool, and then click on the curve where you want the new point. A point is added to the curve. Select the Edit tool, and try moving the new point to make sure it's actually attached to the curve and not just sitting near it. Click on the point and drag it around.

DELETING POINTS/SMOOTHING CURVES

Sometimes, you have part of a glyph that needs smoothing out. You can fiddle with moving points and handles, but sometimes the solution is to actually delete one of the points on the curve in question. By doing so, the curve will adjust itself in a more simplified, generally smoother fashion.

To remove a point, simply choose the Edit tool, select the point you'd like to delete, and press the delete key on your keyboard. The point is removed and the curve where the point was is reshaped accordingly. Image 2 illustrates this process.

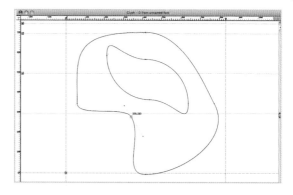

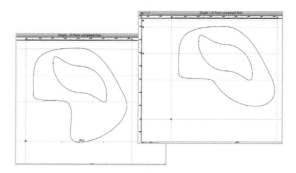

✳ ✳ ✱ *FontLab Tutorial*

CREATING A "P"

Let's create a new glyph to apply some of the skills we've been talking about. Go back to the main window, and double-click on the "P" cell to open up your editing window.

1

Draw a vertical rectangle for the glyph's stem. Click on the rectangle tool and drag from the cap-height line down and to the right to the baseline. After you draw it, the rectangle should be selected. It will be all highlighted in red; if it's not, you can do any of the following to select it: double-click on one of the rectangle's edges; drag the mouse over all of its corner points; or press ctrl-A, which will select everything on the canvas.

2

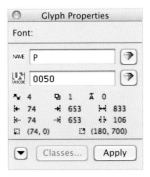

Take a look at the Glyph Properties panel, which will have all sorts of useful information displayed on it. It reports that my glyph (your info will be slightly different, of course, based on where you created your rectangle) starts 74 units to the right of the left sidebearing (that's the 74 next to the little left-pointing arrow); it starts right on the baseline itself—that's the zero in the coordinates (74, 0); it extends horizontally from 74 to 180 (as shown by (180, 700)—its top-rightmost point; and its right sidebearing is 833 units away from the left sidebearing.

3

You should check at this point to make sure the rectangle is pretty much where you want it to be, and that its bottom is exactly on the baseline, and its top is exactly up to the cap height. We know that my rectangle is indeed on the baseline and is exactly up to the cap height by looking at the Glyph Properties panel, but we could also get that information by clicking on each individual point of the rectangle and looking at its coordinates in the editing window. If you need to adjust your rectangle to be in the proper location at the proper height, go ahead and do that now. Remember, you can move individual points by clicking and dragging them, or by clicking on one to select it and then nudging it with the arrow keys on your keyboard. This nudging technique is probably what you want to use if your point is pretty close to where you want it to be. Remember also that you can drag an entire shape by selecting the shape and then either dragging it with the mouse or nudging it with your keyboard's arrow keys.

4

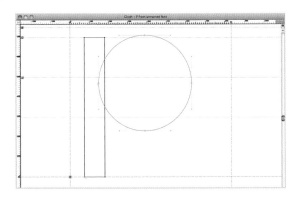

Draw a circle to start your glyph's lobe. Select the oval tool and click and drag from slightly above the cap height to somewhere around two-thirds of the way toward the baseline.

5

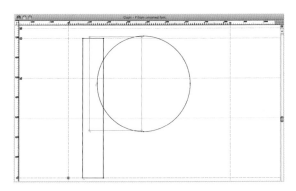

Add another rectangle that runs from near the top point of the circle to near the bottom point of the circle, and close to the left edge of the stem.

6

It's best to avoid aligning two shapes while you're drawing—if the second shape you draw is too close to the first, you'll have a difficult time seeing the different positions of the two. It will be difficult to select the first points because they will be masked by the second shape. That's why I wanted you to draw the new rectangle near the circle's top and bottom points, without getting too close. But now we have to make sure that the rightmost points of the new rectangle coincide with the top and bottom points of the circle.

7

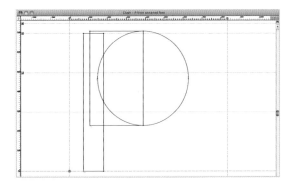

Choose the Edit tool and click on the topmost circle point. Write down its coordinates. Click on the bottommost circlepoint and write down its coordinates. Next, click on the rectangle's rightmost points, one at a time, and nudge them until the coordinates are the same as the circle's points. Your rectangle and circle are now perfectly aligned. Go to the main window to get a preview of what you're doing in the matrix of glyphs.

Continues...

8

A circle by itself wouldn't accomplish what we need for the lobe of a "P"—we need straight lines running horizontally from the top and bottom of the circle to extend the edges. Add the rectangle and circle shapes to make the basic shape of the lobe. Double-click on the new rectangle to select it; then hold the shift key and double-click on the circle. Both should appear selected in red. (If they're not both selected, deselect all and try again.) Now go to the Contour menu and select Transform/Merge Contours. The rectangle and circle merge into one shape.

9

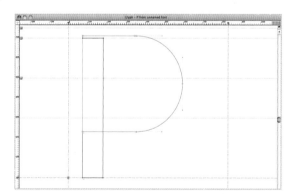

The next step will be easier if you line up this new shape with the left edge of the stem. Click on one of the left edge's points and write down its horizontal coordinate; click on one of the leftmost points of your new shape and see how far away it is from the stem's edge. Now select the entire new shape (double-click on one of its edges) and nudge the entire shape into place.

10

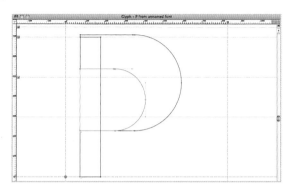

Duplicate the new lobe by double-clicking on it to select it, then press ctrl-C to copy it and ctrl-V to paste it onto the canvas. The copy will appear in a selected state (highlighted red), and will paste itself in place directly on top of the old shape. Double-click on one of its edges and scale it down (grab one of its corner points and drag inward, holding the Shift key to keep the shape proportional) to a reasonable size to be the inner edge of the glyph's lobe.

11

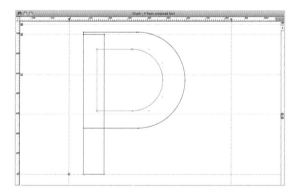

Drag the entire inner shape to approximately the vertical center of the lobe. To make sure the rightmost points of the two shapes are at the same height, select the rightmost point of the outer shape and write down its height coordinate (472 in my case). Now select the rightmost point of the smaller glyph and check out its height coordinate. If it's a couple of units off, select the entire new shape (double-click on it) and nudge it into the proper location with your keyboard. You'll also have to move the inner shape to the right.

12

Subtract the smaller of the two lobe shapes from the larger one. (Select one by double-clicking on one of its edges; and the other by holding down the Shift key and double-clicking on one of its edges.) Once they are both selected, go to the Contour menu and select Transform/Delete Intersection. Check out your handiwork by going back to the main screen for a preview.

13

We wouldn't normally do this step until later in the design process, but I'll run through it now for completeness' sake. (It's often good to keep large shapes independent of one another for a while, for several reasons. For one thing, some of these shapes will be reusable while creating other glyphs, and when they're kept independent, they're easier to copy and paste into other glyphs.) Select both shapes: double-click on one of them, then hold the Shift key while double-clicking the other—they should both be highlighted in red, and go to the Contour menu and select Transform/Merge Contours. You are now the proud owner of a "P" glyph! Congratulations!

FINE POINTS

X

When I first started designing fonts, I thought a proper uppercase "X" was composed of perfectly symmetrical monolines. But upon close examination, we can see that most Xs have subtle variations from symmetrical monolines.

Image 1 shows, from left to right, uppercase sans serif "Xs" from Gibson, Futura, Akzidenz Grotesk, and Avenir. The orange overlays show perfectly symmetrical, monoline strokes—what I used to think a perfect uppercase "X" was composed of. It turns out that a mathematically balanced "X" looks top-heavy, which is why the glyphs in image 1 all rise in part above their mathematically perfect centers.

For serif fonts, there's an additional issue—an optical illusion. When a thick and a thin line cross diagonally, the thin line appears to be too high above the point of intersection. Image 2 is the "X" from Basilia. The upper part of the thin stroke has been shifted to the right to compensate for the optical illusion that would make it seem unbalanced if it were perfectly symmetrical.

✳ ✳ ✳ *FontLab Tutorial*

A PROBLEM OF SCALE

If you find that your P's lobe sits too high on the stem, you have two options for fixing it.

Neither of these strategies is perfect—you will have to manually tweak the lobe to get it to the right size and thickness—but either of them will get you closer to your goal.

2

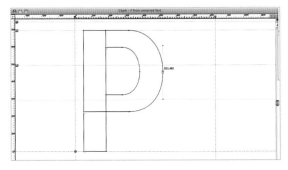

You could fix part of the problem by dragging up the center points of your lobe half as much as you just dragged them down, but there's still a problem with the lobe. You have to select each of the middle points of the lobe, and drag the handles—up for the up-pointing one, and down for the down-pointing one. This smoothes out the shape of the lobe, making it more circular once again.

1

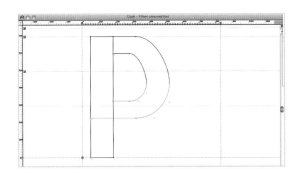

The first option is to drag the lower and middle points of the lobe down to an acceptable position (drag your mouse over the points in question to select them; then drag straight down). This strategy has a serious misshaping problem that is obvious by looking at what happens to your glyph.

3

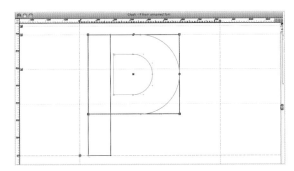

The second strategy is to select the entire lobe (double-click on the inner part of the lobe; hold the Shift key while double-clicking on the outer part), double-click on it to put the shape into transform mode, and then click on the bottom-right corner and drag the entire shape (holding the Shift key to keep it proportional) outward to make it bigger. Of course the problem now is that the lobe is too fat. The solution is to select the inner part of the lobe and scale it up to make the entire lobe thinner.

✳✳✻ *FontLab Tutorial*

MAKING STRAIGHT LINES CURVED AND CURVED LINES STRAIGHT

There will be times you'll be working with a straight line and want to convert it to a curve; conversely, there will be times you'll be working with a curve and want to make it a straight line. FontLab makes it easy to accomplish either of these tasks. I'll show you the straight-to-curved version first, along the practical lines of creating a rounded glyph.

Rounded fonts are generally sans serif, and have, where there would normally be flat caps, rounded caps instead.

2

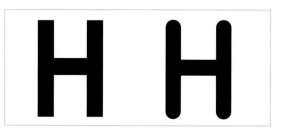

Now let's round the caps. Select the top line of your rectangle (drag the mouse over both of the top two points, or click once on one point and hold the Shift key down while you click once on the second point). Now right-click anywhere on the line you've just selected and choose Convert > To Curves from the pop-up menu. The straight line you drew is now a curve. Deselect everything (ctrl-U). Now click in the middle of your new curve, and drag it slowly upward until you get a cap of the right height and shape. As an example, above are the H from Predicate Bold and Predicate Bold Rounded. They're the same glyph, except the rounded version has rounded caps instead of flat tops. The cap is smoothly connected to the stem.

1

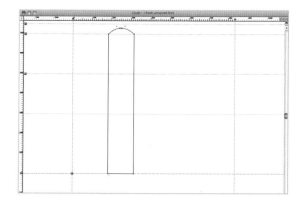

It's easy enough to create rounded caps for your fonts in FontLab. Let's create a quick "I" in your font and give it rounded caps. Get to your main window in FontLab and double-click on the "I" cell in the glyph matrix to open it up in an editing window. Choose the rectangle tool and draw a rectangle from the cap height down to the baseline.

3

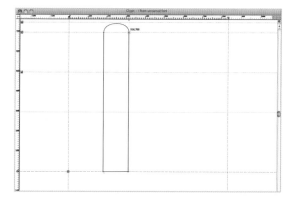

Double-click on each of the top points of your glyph. This straightens out the handle on each point so that it's parallel to the stem, and means that the cap is joined to the stem perfectly smoothly. Repeat the procedure to the bottom of the stem for a well-rounded glyph. To convert the rounded "I" into a flat-bottom, flat-top "I," select the top cap, right-click on it, and choose Convert > To Lines. Do the same to the bottom cap.

Creating composite glyphs

FontLab makes it easy to create composite glyphs—glyphs composed of two or more glyphs, such as "Á", which can be taken to be composed of an "A" and an acute "´".

When you create a new font in FontLab, the program defaults to giving you a template with 229 glyphs that it thinks you should create. Many of these are accented Latin glyphs, including: ÀÁÂÃÄÅÇÈÉÊËÌÍÎÏ ÑÒÓÔÕÖÙÚÛÜ••Žàáâãäå æçèéêëìíîï ñòóôõöùúûü ••ž

✳✳✱ *FontLab Tutorial*
CREATING AN ACCENTED "A" GLYPH

1

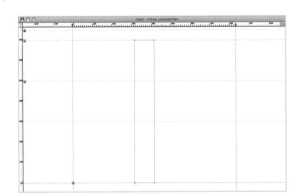

Let's create a makeshift "A" glyph to form an accented "A" glyph. Create a new font or open the font you created in the previous section, then in the main window double click on the "A" cell to open up an editing window. Select the rectangle tool and draw a rectangle from the cap-height line down to the baseline.

2

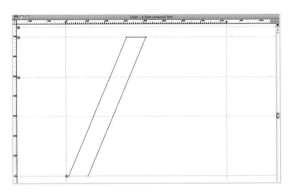

Now select the bottom two nodes on the baseline (drag the mouse over both of them, or click once on one and then hold the Shift key while clicking once on the other one), and drag them to the left. (If you hold the Shift key while dragging them, the nodes will stay on the baseline as you drag.)

3

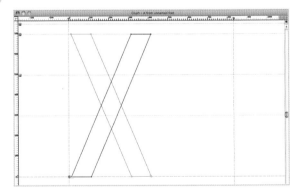

Select the entire shape and copy and paste it. The new copy will lie exactly on top of the old shape and will be selected (colored red). Flip that shape to be a mirror image of the original. Go to the Contour menu, and select Transform > Flip Horizontal. This transforms the shape you've selected as if it were being flipped horizontally across a vertical line.

4

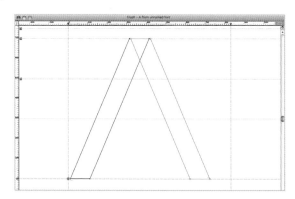

Now move your newly flipped shape to the right. (If you drag it while holding the Shift key, you'll keep the shape aligned on the baseline like its mirrored twin.)

5

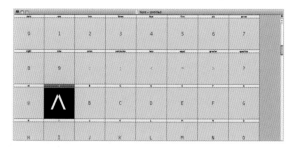

You may at this point notice, if you glance at the main window, that something odd has happened to your glyph-in-progress. The intersection of the two shapes is showing up as a blank spot in your "A."

6

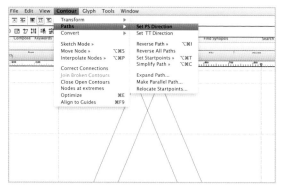

Flipping the shape in step 5 has changed its direction, so that FontLab now renders it differently from other shapes. The cure is to select the flipped shape (double click on its contour), go to the Contour menu, and select Paths > Set PS Direction. If you ever find yourself with glyphs that display with unexpected holes, or appear as something like negative versions of what you expect, try selecting shapes and setting their PS direction.

7

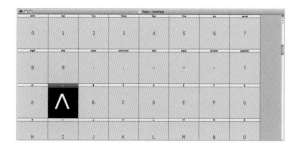

Once you've done this, your glyph displays properly in the main window.

Continues...

8

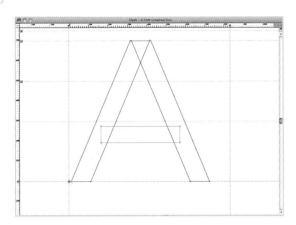

Now you need a crossbar. Make sure the rectangle tool is selected and draw yourself one.

9

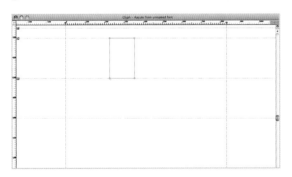

Choose everything (cmd-A) and go to the Contour menu and choose Transform > Merge Contours. This merges all of your separate shapes into one big shape. Now let's draw an acute glyph. Go back to the main window and find the acute cell. Double click on it. In the editing window, draw a rectangle from the cap height line down to about the x-height line, about the same width as the sides of your "A."

10

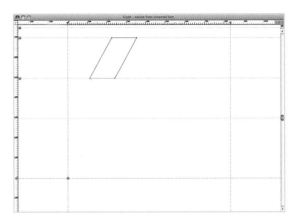

Select the bottom two nodes of the rectangle, and move them to the left.

11

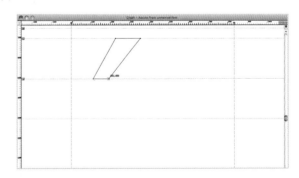

Next, select the bottom rightmost node and move it to the left, to give your acute a taper at its bottom.

12

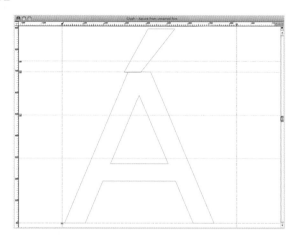

Now we have an "A" and an acute, and armed with these, we can get FontLab to set up a composite A-acute glyph. It won't be perfect, but will be a good starting point. Get back to the main window, and double click on the A-acute cell to open it up in an editing window.

13

tweak your "A"...

and the change shows up in your composite "A"

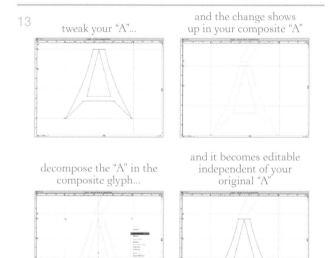

decompose the "A" in the composite glyph...

and it becomes editable independent of your original "A"

FontLab has taken your "A" and your acute and put them together in a reasonable approximation of what an A-acute should look like. Both parts of your new composite are displayed in gray. This means that your "A" and your acute are both live copies—if you make a change to either of the original component glyphs, those changes will be immediately reflected in the composite.

14

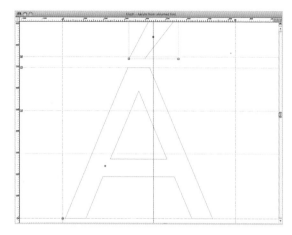

Let's move the acute to a more reasonable position. Click on it and drag to move it.

15

Á Á Á Á
Á Á Á Á

You now have an A-acute! Let's look at what an A with an acute looks like in some well-known fonts. In the top row from left to right are: Myriad Pro, Helvetica, Futura, and Frutiger. In the bottom row from left to right are: Akzidenz Grotesk, Verdana, Gibson, and Gill Sans.

VARIETIES OF ACUTE ACCENTS

One thing you'll notice upon examining fonts is that most accents are not bottom-centered with their corresponding glyphs. That is, for instance, the bottom of the acute that sits over an "A" is well to the left of the center of the "A." This creates a balance of the two components—since the acute slants to the right, starting it to the left of the center of the "A" means that it is actually visually centered with the "A."

Another thing you'll notice is that acutes come in a lot of different slants, sizes, and distances from their corresponding glyphs. In the top row of image 1, you can see that some of the acutes are shorter than others, some are more monoline, and some are farther away from their "A"s. There is no exact science to this—play with the sizing, shape, and placement of your accents until you find something that works well with your font.

Also, know that you are not constrained by the accents you create. If you need to tweak an acute for an individual glyph, you can do that easily in FontLab, and you won't be alone in doing so. In Minion Pro (the top row of image 1), the acutes over the lowercase letters are clearly different from the acutes over the uppercase. In Akzidenz Grotesk (the bottom row of image 1), the acutes over lower-and uppercase letters look the same from a distance, but upon closer inspection are seen to be different.

It is common practice to have a completely different acute to be paired with lowercase glyphs (often particularly dramatically different in serif fonts). Also, tweaking an individual acute to accommodate its relationship with another glyph is not unheard of.

To make the acute in your A-acute glyph not a live copy, you can select it, right click on it, and choose "Decompose" from the pop-up menu. This turns it from a live copy to a plain shape in your composite glyph. After decomposing the acute in image 2, it becomes not a link to a glyph, but merely a shape in this glyph; you can make changes to it independently from any changes to the acute glyph.

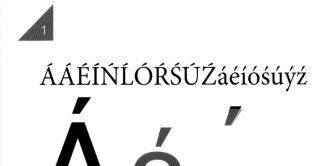

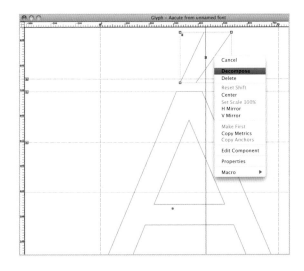

FINE POINTS

Little things

Sometimes it's the little things that make all the difference.

You might think that you can just take a comma, raise it up, and you've got a right single quote ready to go. You might also think that the dots under the question mark and exclamation mark are identical. Actually, in the majority of cases you'd be right, but some fonts don't take the easy road here. Check out the little differences in Minion Pro that make a big difference in the overall scheme of things. In image 1, on the left we have the comma in black with the right single quote overlaid in magenta. On the right we have the dot from the question mark overlaid in magenta on the dot from the exclamation point in black.

Again, you might think that a hyphen and a minus sign would be identical, but in many fonts that's not the case. Image 2 shows the two glyphs in Minion Pro, along with en and em dashes for comparison's sake.

hyphen

minus sign

en dash

em dash

Spacing

Sidebearings are the imaginary lines that denote the left and right boundaries of a glyph. Imagine that there are boxes around every glyph of a font, dictating to the software that uses a font where to begin and end placing characters.

The top row of image 1 shows the sidebearings for some glyphs in Myriad Pro. The bottom row shows what happens when those glyphs are placed side by side according to those sidebearings—lovely, readable text.

Careful placement of those boxes mean that when your glyphs are placed next to one another, the spacing of those letters is generally optimal—that is, the spacing works as well as it can for the greatest number of pairs of adjacent letters.

This is what good sidebearings do for your font. They make it easy for software to display text using your font in a well-set way. If you created a font with sidebearings that were the same for each glyph, the result would be a pretty difficult-to-use font. Check out what happens to Helvetica when you apply constant sidebearings instead of the well-thought-out sidebearings its creators actually gave it (image 2).

With its original sidebearings (top row), even this ungainly word displays reasonably well. Note what happens, though, when the original sidebearings are discarded and replaced with sidebearings that are exactly the same from glyph to glyph (middle row). The spacing between the letters is terrible. The third example shows Helvetica with its regular sidebearings, complete with kerning (bottom row). Kerning, which we'll be addressing in the next section, adds additional instructions with the font to space specific letter pairs differently than the default sidebearings allow.

As far as dealing with sidebearings is concerned, there are, in broad terms, three sorts of sides of glyphs: straight (vertical) sides, diagonal sides, and rounded sides. Straight sides of glyphs have, as a rule of thumb, the largest sidebearings. Rounded sides generally have somewhat smaller sidebearings. And diagonal sides of glyphs, generally speaking, have the smallest sidebearings.

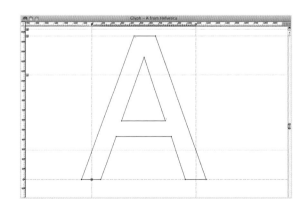

Helvetica with its own sidebearings

Helvetica with constant sidebearings

Helvetica with its own sidebearings and kerning

One glyph can have two different types of sides: "D" glyphs have a straight side on the left and a rounded side on the right; "K" glyphs have a straight side on the left and a diagonal side on the right. Some glyphs don't fall neatly into our three categories: "T" glyphs barely have sides at all, although generally speaking they can fall into the diagonal side category; "U" glyphs generally have straight sides that round slightly at the bottom. When setting sidebearings for the "U," you might want to make them a little closer than, say, an "N," with its perfectly straight sides.

The art of setting sidebearings (and it is an art as much as a science, to be sure) is to try to equalize as best you can the whitespace between adjacent glyphs. Think about Helvetica's "A" and "N." If the "A" had the same wide sidebearings as the "N," the "A" would look farther apart from other glyphs—the amount of whitespace created by the slope of the sides of the "A" is much greater than the whitespace created by the vertical sides of the "N," so that other adjacent glyphs appear to be closer to the "N" than to the "A."

Looking at certain letter pairs, such as "AV," you might be tempted to create your "A" with negative sidebearings—that is, sidebearings that intrude into the actual shape of the glyph (image 3). This is entirely allowable in a font, and would solve the problem of the distance between the "A" and the "V" when they're laid out next to each other (image 4).

Unfortunately, it would create more problems than it solved. Look what happens to the "AJ" pair in image 5 with this new sidebearing setup. The "A" and the "J" are far too close to one another.

Sidebearings are a general solution to the issue of spacing letters—they provide good spacing for the greatest number of possible cases. They will fail for certain pairs of letters—you simply can't help it. Kerning is the cure for fixing specific cases. We'll see much more about kerning in the next section.

For your reference, there is a table on the following page detailing the sidebearings of some well-known sans serif fonts, given in generic FontLab units (image 6).

AVERSE

AJAR

SPACING FOR OTHER GLYPHS

I've been talking only about setting sidebearings for your A–Z glyphs, but don't neglect all of the other glyphs in your font. Even the space glyph needs attention as far as sidebearings go. I remember developing my first font, and thinking something was wrong with it when I used it to typeset a passage of text, even though I couldn't put my finger on what was wrong. Finally it dawned on me: I had kept FontLab's default sidebearings for my space glyph, and these were far too wide for the font. Words had gaps between them that were not in keeping with the character of the font. Bringing the right sidebearing closer to the left solved the problem.

Continues...

Glyph	Akzidenz Grotesk		Candara		Century Gothic		Franklin Gothic		Frutiger		Gill Sans		Helvetica		Mundo Sans		Myriad Pro		Univers	
	LSB	RSB	LSB	RSB	LSB	RSB	LSB	RSB	LSB	RSB	LSB	RSB	LSB	RSB	LSB	RSB	LSB	RSB	LSB	RSB
A	10	12	11	11	49	49	7	7	12	12	0	0	30	25	2	5	25	23	9	10
a	32	14	88	122	107	159	68	135	46	75	55	32	82	44	34	15	35	61	53	74
B	77	48	188	99	183	112	171	84	83	76	154	43	151	82	91	45	76	41	95	59
b	65	38	122	99	165	99	157	79	80	46	121	72	118	78	77	39	69	37	81	46
C	49	22	99	66	111	116	85	41	53	31	100	92	90	86	43	34	36	32	56	37
c	39	27	99	55	105	113	78	58	38	28	78	78	59	48	41	22	38	28	39	33
D	78	50	188	99	179	106	171	85	83	61	156	96	165	100	92	43	76	37	88	45
d	39	65	99	133	109	161	79	157	46	80	90	118	56	134	41	75	37	69	54	74
E	79	27	188	66	180	75	171	68	94	71	154	59	175	105	91	40	76	37	75	75
e	39	38	99	99	104	105	78	79	46	46	84	68	72	89	41	42	38	36	51	51
F	78	11	188	44	179	77	171	33	83	46	156	60	175	57	91	37	76	48	79	49
f	11	0	22	0	79	39	7	-21	21	14	18	-94	28	34	13	-51	14	-39	16	-6
G	50	71	99	133	117	101	85	143	53	88	104	138	99	152	43	70	36	57	68	90
g	41	65	66	33	100	144	52	-16	46	80	0	12	61	139	30	3	38	69	51	77
H	79	78	188	188	177	178	171	170	94	94	154	154	161	152	92	94	76	75	90	89
h	66	62	122	130	156	144	157	157	80	80	125	125	132	134	77	71	73	70	90	89
I	67	67	188	188	158	158	171	170	89	89	156	156	201	167	93	95	76	76	89	89
i	69	62	111	91	90	89	150	151	86	86	117	117	132	140	72	71	62	62	83	82
J	9	78	22	166	86	179	0	157	21	91	-125	156	35	147	-91	97	4	69	20	103
j	-23	65	10	91	-64	93	-124	147	-16	86	-10	127	-38	143	-85	73	-45	60	6	78
K	67	1	188	22	179	40	171	37	94	16	156	0	128	8	93	5	76	-10	92	1
k	65	-14	122	11	155	-12	157	35	80	19	129	-43	156	8	77	2	73	-10	79	2
L	68	17	188	22	179	54	171	26	88	20	154	21	137	138	91	2	76	21	93	27
l	67	65	122	144	135	135	157	157	92	92	133	134	156	40	77	75	73	75	92	91
M	68	66	144	166	112	112	171	170	90	90	150	147	132	133	87	83	58	58	92	92
m	64	63	100	130	155	139	157	157	79	78	121	121	151	147	78	73	69	70	88	87
N	78	78	188	188	180	180	171	170	88	88	160	145	132	134	92	87	76	76	99	99
n	64	65	111	130	156	144	157	157	80	80	125	125	156	157	77	72	69	70	90	84
O	51	50	99	99	115	116	85	86	53	53	92	91	59	82	43	44	36	37	59	59
o	40	39	99	99	104	104	78	79	46	46	76	73	80	81	42	42	38	38	56	55
P	76	11	188	66	178	115	171	47	83	28	143	20	118	78	92	32	76	41	88	31
p	65	39	111	99	158	106	157	78	80	46	117	70	175	94	78	40	69	38	81	46
Q	47	6	99	133	106	158	78	157	53	53	90	91	60	134	41	77	38	69	66	17
q	39	65	99	64	117	118	85	86	46	80	72	117	80	81	43	35	36	32	47	79
R	78	10	188	66	187	115	171	102	83	30	160	0	137	24	93	13	76	23	93	19
r	65	7	100	-10	103	-37	157	21	80	24	141	-2	180	79	78	0	69	15	86	58
S	37	49	99	99	27	132	21	83	47	47	84	66	66	74	43	41	42	43	55	61
s	31	32	86	91	54	91	21	64	34	34	84	81	96	96	35	34	39	40	42	42
T	11	14	22	22	33	32	21	20	11	11	35	35	23	48	3	3	-1	-1	14	13
t	16	33	44	55	87	53	-1	15	7	30	0	2	33	26	15	10	18	26	9	27
U	76	76	166	166	184	183	150	150	90	90	125	123	128	149	84	84	75	75	97	97
u	64	67	130	122	138	155	157	157	80	80	125	127	170	152	70	69	70	69	90	89
V	11	12	11	11	67	68	7	7	6	6	0	0	52	32	4	4	4	-3	17	17
v	12	11	44	44	53	58	24	25	11	11	6	8	11	22	8	7	13	10	16	15
W	18	18	11	11	96	96	39	39	2	2	0	2	37	28	8	11	15	8	8	8
w	11	10	44	44	9	9	38	39	12	12	0	0	18	38	5	-3	18	15	11	11
X	21	20	11	11	69	68	5	5	8	8	4	4	42	34	4	8	25	25	20	20
x	9	9	55	55	-7	-8	7	7	10	10	0	0	11	31	7	8	8	12	19	18
Y	14	14	22	22	63	63	-20	-20	11	11	0	0	42	15	0	0	13	1	2	1
y	9	12	44	44	39	25	11	0	7	16	0	0	21	24	6	5	9	7	16	15
Z	18	33	99	99	56	85	56	47	32	41	25	37	47	47	4	13	18	17	40	39
z	13	28	99	99	9	4	68	55	43	43	23	25	52	76	4	7	30	31	23	22

FINE POINTS

Terminals

The ends of many strokes in serif fonts end, obviously, in serifs. But not all of them do. Two other stroke endings are spurs and tails (highlighted in image 1). There are also terminals.

There is an incredible amount of variation in the types of terminals that font designers create. Image 2 shows the variety of terminals in the "y" glyphs of (from left to right) Clarendon Text, Georgia, Times New Roman, BasiliaT, Minion Pro, Goudy Old Style, Gentium, Museo Slab, and Rockwell.

Why don't font designers simply draw a serifed bottom to all of these glyphs? The problem is one of balance and flow within a body of text. A fully serifed "y" is simply not visually well-balanced. In the flow of text, the bottom of a fully serifed "y" is somewhat spindly and its wide serif sitting in whitespace draws attention to this. Minion Pro's "y" is shown on the left of image 3; on the right is the same glyph but with a serifed bottom, created by the author. Notice how the version with the serifed bottom is unbalanced when magnified, and at normal text sizes is at once spindly and draws too much attention to its bottom.

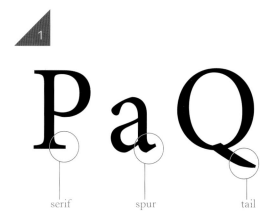

serif   spur   tail

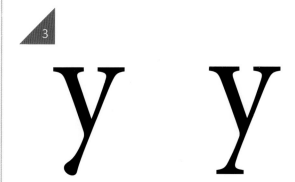

Kerning

Kerning is all about pairs of glyphs. You set sidebearings for each individual glyph one at a time; you set the kerning between two glyphs at a time. Remember our troublesome pair of glyphs from the previous section: "AV"? Once you've set your sidebearings for each of these glyphs, so that the "A" and the "V" work as well as they can for the majority of glyphs with which they combine, the "AV" combination itself will be problematic, since the two glyphs sit too far apart from one another. Kerning is the solution. You do all of your kerning work in FontLab, and then that kerning information is stored with the font, and is available for use by word-processing and page-layout programs that use your font.

✳✳✱ *FontLab Tutorial*

KERNING

If you've set your sidebearings well, your kerning job will be easier. But no amount of sidebearing-setting will spare you the necessity of kerning, so let's wade into the fun.

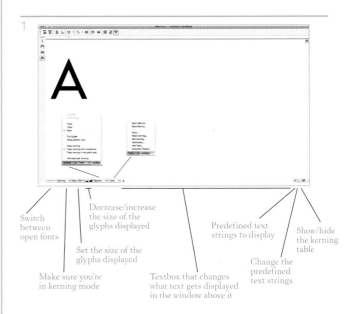

Switch between open fonts

Decrease/increase the size of the glyphs displayed

Set the size of the glyphs displayed

Make sure you're in kerning mode

Predefined text strings to display

Textbox that changes what text gets displayed in the window above it

Change the predefined text strings

Show/hide the kerning table

To start kerning, make sure a font is open, click once on the "A" cell in the main window, and then click on the New Metrics Window button in the toolbar. The "A" will now appear at a large size in a brand-new metrics window. (Whatever glyph you have highlighted in the main window will display in any new metrics window you open.)

2

Since kerning is done in pairs, we need another glyph in this window. Click in the textbox at the bottom of your Metrics window and type a "V" after the "A."

3

Although you could do all of your kerning with just two glyphs displayed at a time, I find it much more helpful to have a string of glyphs displayed. Even though I'm focused on kerning a pair at a time, seeing other glyphs at work in the same context makes it so that I'm kerning holistically. It's altogether too easy to kern pairs in isolation that subsequently don't fit with the rest of the font. So let's type in a few more letters.

4

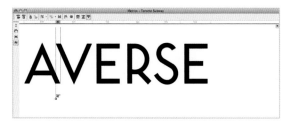

In the font I opened (Toronto Subway), the black line under the "A," along with the blue bar above it with a negative number in it, tells you that the "AV" pair has already been kerned by this font's creator. (The other pairs in this set of glyphs have not been kerned, because the font's sidebearings were well placed.) If you click on the "V" in the Metrics window, a line (denoting its left sidebearing) and handle appear, showing you where the kerning between the "A" and the "V" exists.

5

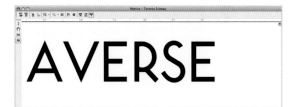

If there were no kerning set, the line would be at the junction of the right sidebearing of the "A" and the left sidebearing of the "V." Kerning instructions tell the font how far to deviate from this junction of sidebearings.

Continues...

6

If you have the "V" selected in the Metrics window, you can either drag it directly to the left or right to change its kerning with the "A," or you can drag the handle at the bottom of the "V" 's left sidebearing line. If you drag it to the left of the sidebearings junction, you have standard kerning—bringing two glyphs closer together, despite what their sidebearings would dictate. If you drag it instead to the right, bringing the glyphs farther apart from one another, you have positive kerning. The "AV" pair is here positively kerned.

7

If you click on the drop-down list at the bottom of the Metrics window with numeric values in it, you can easily change the display size of your kerning examples. It's important to check your font's kerning at multiple sizes, and to decide early on at which size the kerning is meant to look its best.

POSITIVE KERNING

Although it is perfectly allowable in FontLab, purists might argue that positive kerning is not the best practice. Generally speaking, your sidebearings should do the work of adequately separating your glyphs from one another, and so kerning is thought of as the way to bring individual pairs of glyphs closer to one another, not to separate them further. Purists' concerns aside, I've used positive kerning in several of my fonts, to, I think, good effect. If you find yourself making more than the occasional positive kern, it might be time to go back and rethink your sidebearings; but as an occasional tool, I see nothing wrong with the practice.

KERNING AT DIFFERENT SIZES

In most of these screenshots, I've had the Metrics window set to display my glyphs at a very large size. I do a great deal of my kerning at large display sizes, in part because I create a lot of display fonts; that is, my fonts are often meant to be used at very large sizes, so it makes sense to kern them at very large sizes. If you're creating a font that's meant to be often used at small sizes, you should spend a lot of your time kerning at small sizes in FontLab. One danger of kerning such a font at large sizes is that you're probably going to kern glyphs much more closely together than you would otherwise—the larger the size, the greater the whitespace between glyphs appears.

FINE POINTS
When monoline isn't

Often even a symmetrical, relatively monoline sans serif font will have many subtle irregular features that add visual interest and typographic nuance.

Let's take a look at Helvetica—the paragon, many would argue, of simple typographic elegance. Helvetica's "b" is not genuinely monoline; that is, it is not exactly the same width at all of its points. You can see this more clearly by overlaying a genuinely monoline version of the "b" on top of the real "b" (image 1).

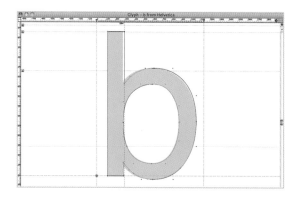

Note that the real "b" narrows where its lobe connects with its stem. Also, the stem itself is not the same width from the top to the bottom—it gets narrower at the bottom, beneath where the bowl connects with it. This gives the glyph some extra whitespace at that junction, which means that there's more definition there at small type sizes.

Helvetica's "n" possesses some interesting characteristics as well (image 2). Notably, once again, its stem isn't the same width through its entire height—it thins out at the top junction, to give more definition to the junction. Also, the shoulder of the "n"—the curved top of the glyph—is not exactly vertically aligned. It skews to the right, which gives the shape a little interest and unexpected visual balance.

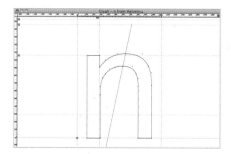

Zooming into Helvetica's "M" in image 3 shows an even subtler deviation from its monoline appearance. At the junction of its left stem and diagonal stroke, the stem veers ever so slightly inward. Without this tiny notch, at small type sizes, the junction appears too thick.

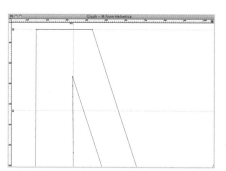

✳✳✳ *FontLab Tutorial*
KERNING CLASSES

FontLab has a built-in mechanism for making kerning a little easier: kerning classes. The idea is brilliant—if you have several glyphs that have the same basic shape, you should be able to kern just one of them with other glyphs, and then have the same kerning apply to the similarly shaped glyphs. This is just what kerning classes allow you to do. You put a key glyph into the class, along with a group of similarly shaped glyphs; you kern the key glyph with other glyphs in the font, and then FontLab does some magic behind the scenes to apply that kerning to the similarly shaped glyphs.

1

Open a font you've been working on, or create a new font. For the purposes of the following demonstrations, you should create at least the following glyphs: A, Aacute, Agrave, Acircumflex (which means you should really have acute, grave, and circumflex glyphs created as well), V, D, and Eth. (Don't worry about making them pretty—we just need basic shapes to get some points across.)

2

Assuming you have a font at the ready, the first thing you need to do in order to set up kerning classes is to make sure your Classes panel is showing. Go to the Window menu and select Panels > Classes.

3

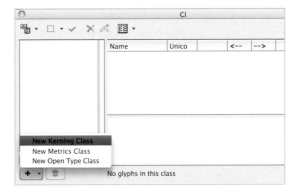

Now click on the button with the plus sign on it (in the lower left of the panel), and choose New Kerning Class. FontLab creates an empty kerning class for you, called, by default, "_kern1".

4

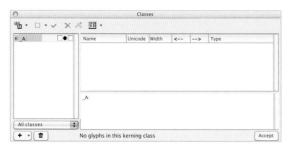

Let's change the name to "_A", since we'll be creating a kerning class for all of the A-shaped glyphs in our font. Click on the "_kern1" text in the lower-right panel; select the existing text, and type "_A" in its place. Keep the underscore in the name. When you're done, make sure to click on the Accept button to finalize your changes. The name will change in the left-hand panel. Also, click both checkboxes in the left pane—this tells FontLab to kern both sides of each glyph in the class.

5

Now we have to do two things: specify a key glyph for the kerning class—the glyph with which you will be kerning—and then specify which other glyphs will be in the kerning class and will inherit the key glyph's kerning instructions. In our case, we want the key glyph to be the "A," and the other class's glyphs to be (for starters) Aacute and Agrave. This means that every glyph we kern with the "A" will also get kerned in the same way with Aacute and Agrave. Click in the lower-right panel, and, after the colon in "_A:" type (without quotes): "A Aacute Agrave". Click on the Accept button to finalize this change. (You can also drag glyphs from the main window into the class panel.)

6

The "A Aacute Agrave" string is three glyph names (this is what FontLab names these glyphs), separated by spaces. Order is important here: the first glyph name in a kerning class definition is the key glyph—the glyph from which the other glyphs in the class take their kerning instructions.

Let's see how our hard work manifests itself. Open a new metrics window (Window > New Metrics Window) and type into the text box (without quotes): "AV/Aacute/V/Agrave/V".

7

You'll no doubt notice the odd formatting I've supplied here. You can provide FontLab glyph names in the metrics window text box by typing a forward slash "/" followed by the name of the glyph. When you're dealing with standard, unaccented glyphs, you can just type that glyph name in without a slash, because the name is a single character. (The name of "A" is "A".) But if you type in "Aacute" without a slash, FontLab will think you're trying to type in a six-glyph string: "A" "a" "c" "u" "t" "e". The slash tells FontLab to translate everything after it (until the next slash or a space) as a glyph name. The string I've provided for this example could just as well have been "/A/V/Aacute/V/Agrave/V", but I gave you the option with the least amount of typing involved.

Continues…

8

FontLab displays your string of glyphs in the metrics window. Four of the glyphs are a blue-purplish color—these are the glyphs that will get their kerning instructions from the kerning class you've created, and so the different coloring is to remind you that you don't have to manipulate these glyphs in this context.

Let's try kerning the "AV" pair. Click on the first "V" and drag it slowly to the left, getting it closer to the "A"—in my example, it's 98 units closer. This is giving the instruction to your font: "whenever there's an 'AV' pair displayed, the 'V' will be moved 98 units closer to the 'A'." (This is not reciprocal—a "VA" pair has to be kerned separately in order for the "A" to move closer to the "V" in such a pairing. Order matters in kerning!)

9

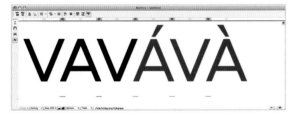

Because you have put your Aacute and Agrave in your _A kerning class, the "V" to the right of these glyphs is moved 98 units closer to them as well, automatically! Now let's kern the "VA" combination. Type the following string into the text box in your metrics window (without quotes): "VAV/Aacute/V/Agrave". Drag the first "A" to the left the same number of units as the "V" was kerned closer to the "A" in the previous example. (The value will be displayed in two places in the metrics window: above the glyph in a horizontal bar, and also, if the glyph is selected in the metrics window, next to the handle displayed below the glyph.)

10

Again, because you have put your Aacute and Agrave in your _A kerning class, all of these glyphs are moved 98 units closer to the "V." Remember, you have to specify which glyphs go in the kerning class. If you add the Acircumflex to the text box in the metrics window, you'll see that it is not properly kerned, because, even though it has the same shape as your other A glyphs, we didn't add it to the kerning class.

11

If we add it, even after the fact, it gets properly kerned along with the rest of the As.

FINE POINTS
Unicase

I once developed a logo using all capital letters for the company name, with a lowercase tagline just below it. The company loved it, except they wanted—no, they needed--the company name to be in lowercase. Oh, those pesky ascenders and descenders! Naturally, reformatting the new logo to accommodate the tagline was a challenge (image 1).

One thing I could have tried was using a unicase font: a font where all the lowercase and uppercase letters sit on the baseline and rise to the exact same height. There are no ascenders or descenders in unicase fonts, which makes them less challenging to typeset for certain applications. Unicase fonts are specialty fonts—a little use of them goes a long way, and you would almost certainly not want to set large tracts of text in unicase.

There are no hard and fast rules about how to create a unicase font, but often these fonts have lowercase "a," "e," "n," and "r" glyphs drawn to cap height. Many other unicase glyphs are ambiguous as to whether or not they are upper- or lowercase: "c," "f," "k," "m," "o," "s," "u," "v," "w," "x," and "z" in particular are easy to create as ambiguously cased.

Image 2 gives samples of Superfly, Strenuous BL, and Boldesqo Serif 4F, to show off some lovely unicase fonts. In image 3, the unicase font Superfly (right) is placed next to Myriad Pro (left) to show the three heights of Myriad's lowercase glyphs against the one height of Superfly's.

REGULARCO
the company that does regular stuff in a regular way

regularco
the company that does regular stuff in a regular way

regularco
the company that does regular stuff in a regular way

SUPERFLY
UNICASE ABEFGPQE

STRENUOUS BL
UNICASE ABEFGPQE

BOLDESQO SERIF 4F
UNICASE ABEFGJPQE

abcdefghijklmnopqrstuvwxyz ABCDEFGHIJKLMNOPQRSTUVWXYZ

✱✱✱ *FontLab Tutorial*
KERNING ONE SIDE OF A GLYPH

You can also create kerning classes that respect only one side of a glyph. This comes in handy for glyphs that share a common shape on one side; for instance, depending on the font, "B," "D," "E," "F," "H," "K," "L," "M," "N," "P," and "R" might all have the same left-side shape, namely a vertical stem of the same height. It would save you a great deal of work not to have to kern all of these left sides individually with every other glyph. Let's tackle a similar issue on a smaller scale with the "D" and "Eth" glyphs.

The "Eth" is one of those rare letters that you may never have seen, but it is used, most notably, in Icelandic and Old English. It comes in an uppercase and lowercase version. The uppercase version looks like a "D" with a horizontal stroke midway through its stem. The image below shows (from left to right and from top to bottom) "Ds" and "Eths" from Myriad Pro, Minion Pro, Pluto, Museo Slab, Marydale, and Designation.

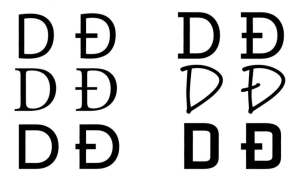

1

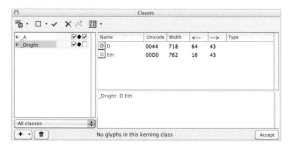

Let's create a new kerning class. Click on the plus sign in the lower-left pane of the Classes panel and select New Kerning Class. Rename it "_Dright" in the lower-right pane and click Accept. Now type (without quotes) "D Eth" in the upper-right pane, and click "Accept" again. This time, instead of checking off both checkboxes in the left pane next to your class name, click only the left checkbox to create a class that groups together glyphs with the same right-side shape. Think of it this way: the left checkbox means that the glyphs in your class are all considered to be the same as the left-side members of kerning pairs; thus the right sides of them all get kerned the same way.

2

Get back to your metrics window and type (without quotes) "DV/Eth/V" in the text box. You can see by the blue "V" that you've set up your kerning class the right way—the second "V" is not meant to be kerned independently of the first "DV" pair—kern that first pair, and the Eth-"V" pair will get kerned automatically, on the right-hand side of the "D" and "Eth." Drag the first "V" to the left, closer to the "D." You'll see that the "Eth-V" pair is similarly kerned, automatically.

3

Type "DA/Eth/A" into the text box of the metrics window, and drag the first "A" closer to the "D." Same result—the "Eth-A" pair is kerned automatically based on the "DA" pair.

4

Since we set up this kerning class to be one-sided (on the right side), the left sides of the pairs are still independent of one another. Type (without quotes) "ADA/Eth" into the text box of the metrics window, and drag the "D" to the left to be uncomfortably close to the first "A." Note that the "A-Eth" pair remains unkerned, because our kerning class of the "D" and the "Eth" is a right-side only class. Since we have just kerned the left side of our "D", our kerning class is not a factor here, which is just as it should be—the left sides of the "D" and "Eth" are not the same, as there is a horizontal stroke protruding out of the "Eth."

FINE POINTS
The ends of curves

A chronic concern when designing sans serif fonts is what to do with the ends of glyphs that come out of curves, i.e., the ends of glyphs such as "S" and "C." Where should they stop, and at what angle from the vertical or horizontal axes?

Different fonts handle these choices differently. Gill Sans (top row of image 1) cuts off its "S" parts at totally parallel to the vertical axis. In fact, it does this for all of its glyphs with curved ends, except, curiously, its "r." (This is curious because most sans serif fonts cut their "r"s off vertically, so you'd expect Gill Sans, with all other ends cut off vertically, to have the same trait for its "r.") Futura (middle row) cuts off its "S" parts at an oblique angle. It treats its "G," "e," "r," and "s" likewise, but then gives its "C," "c," and "f" a vertical cut. Helvetica (bottom row) gives horizontal cuts to most of its glyphs. Its "y," "t," "r," and "f" are notable exceptions, with vertical cuts.

How do you decide what to do with your glyphs? Well, one thing to keep in mind is that strictly vertical cuts will make your glyphs easier to kern—they will hang together nicely by virtue of their clean, straight, uniform edges. However, in isolation, these vertical cuts can look ungainly. In the end, there's no magic formula for deciding which way to go. Experiment, and when in doubt, reference what some of your favorite fonts do.

1

S CGSacefrst

S CGScfers

S CGSacefrsty

Adding OpenType features

A BRIEF HISTORY OF FONT FORMATS

In the beginning there was Postscript. Adobe developed the Postscript programming language in the 1980s as a way to mathematically describe the content of a printable page. A scalable, vector font format came out of the Postscript language, called Type 1. Type 1 fonts quickly became the de facto font format; some of them are still in circulation today, distinguishable by the slew of files needed to make them work—multiple font files per font were needed, with extensions such as .pfb, .pfm, .afm, and .inf. The success of Type 1 prompted Apple and Microsoft to collaborate on a competitor font format that they called TrueType. TrueType eventually became the new de facto font format—for one very big reason, because they worked easily in Microsoft Windows, whereas Type 1 fonts required a third-party program to allow them to work in Windows.

The first version of Minion I ever saw had four font files for each family member: Minion Bold had one font file for Latin glyphs; one for small caps, ligatures, and different figures (called "Expert"); one for ornaments; and one for Cyrillic glyphs. Similarly, Minion had Bold Italic, Minion Book, Minion Book Italic, etc. That's a lot of files.

The problem was that in the olden days of Type 1, font files could contain only 256 glyphs. So if you wanted to include "extra" glyphs such as ligatures, you had to create an entirely new font file to contain those glyphs. Worse than the bloat of extra files, programs generally had no way of knowing that these separate font files composed an actual family. It was up to the user to know that these files with ligatures existed, and know how to use them.

We are now in the golden age of font formats. We have at our disposal the OpenType font format, which was created in the mid-1990s by Adobe and Microsoft, but took a long time to gain acceptance by consumers. Nowadays, even non-savvy users are used to fonts with OpenType's .otf file extension; and that, along with the benefits the format gives font creators and users alike, is a good reason to generate and sell your fonts in OpenType format.

What are the benefits of OpenType? An OpenType font can contain tens of thousands of glyphs. OpenType fonts make it easy to support multiple languages in a single font—it's not uncommon for a professional OpenType font to have Latin glyphs along with a full complement of Greek and Cyrillic glyphs in a single file. OpenType also makes it easy to include advanced typographical features in a font— features such as ligatures (both standard and discretionary), stylistic alternates, and small caps.

LIGATURES

What is a ligature? A ligature is basically two (or more) letterforms joined together to create a single form—in the language of font creation, a ligature is two (or more) glyphs combined in an artistic way into a single glyph.

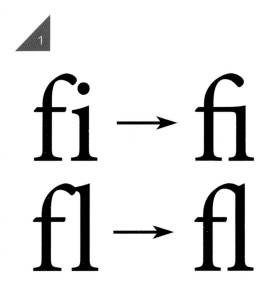

The most famous ligatures are the "fi" and "fl" glyphs. In many fonts, the dot of the "i" trespasses dangerously close to the top of the "f," impedes readability, and is aesthetically unappealing. So font designers often create a single combined "fi" glyph that sits in for the "f-i" pair of glyphs, and generally, the "fi" standard ligature drops the dot of the "i" and moves the base of the "i" under the protective hood of the "f." The case is similar with the "f-l" pair of glyphs—in many fonts, this pairing will bring the "l" crashing into the overhang of the "f," creating aesthetic problems. Font designers will often create an "fl" ligature that designs the collision in an artistic fashion. In the left-hand column in image 1 are Minion Pro glyphs set without ligatures, and in the right-hand column are Minion Pro's standard ligatures in action.

Fonts can also have discretionary ligatures. A discretionary ligature is a combined set of glyphs that is not geometrically necessary, but is nonetheless aesthetically interesting. A usual suspect in many professional fonts is the "st" ligature. As you can see from image 2, there is nothing inherent in the geometry of the "s-t" combination that screams out "shapes are crashing into one another—create a ligature here!" But there is a neat way to connect the two letters that adds visual interest and gives a unique flavor to the font. The wisdom is that generally you'll use a standard ligature when typesetting a document, but occasionally you'll use a discretionary ligature to add spice to your typography. (Using the "st" ligature everywhere in a dense block of text would probably be quite distracting to the reader, but using it in one place on, say, a wedding invitation, might add flair.)

The top two rows of image 3 show a simple discretionary ligature in my font Zurdo. I thought about making it a standard ligature, as the geometry of the "g-g" pair almost demands a melding of the two glyphs. But I decided that there might be instances where one didn't want the melded "gg" ligature, so I made it discretionary. There's no hard and fast rule about which ligatures should be made standard and which should be discretionary; you'll have to use your best judgment when creating your font. The bottom two rows of image 3 show examples from the font Aeronaut, which is a more traditional instance of discretionary ligatures. There's nothing inherent in the geometry of the glyph pairs that need combining, but the font's designer created flourished connections between them, for discretionary use.

2

st → st
ct → ct

3

leggings
leggings

quiddichgame
quiddichgame

✳✳✳ *FontLab Tutorial*
CREATING STANDARD LIGATURES

How do you create standard ligatures in OpenType fonts? There are two steps: First, create the standard ligature glyph. Second, create the OpenType code in the font that tells other programs that this standard ligature is available.

FontLab provides you with cells for "fi" and "fl" ligatures, but if you want to create others, you have to do so manually, and this tutorial will show you how.

2

If you have a very large font, and are worried about finding the new glyph you're about to create, check off the Mark New Glyphs box—FontLab will apply a color to the cell of the new glyph, so that it will stand out in the main window's glyph matrix.

1

Go to the Glyph menu and select Generate Glyphs. Type in the two characters you'd like to combine into a single ligature glyph, separated by an underscore. (The underscore naming convention is just that: a convention, but one I suggest you stick to.) FontLab previews the two characters to be combined.

3

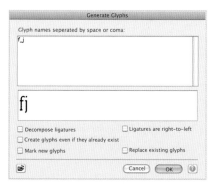

Uncheck the Create Glyphs Even If They Exist box, because it will overwrite any glyph that already exists with the same name as one you're trying to create. If you want to overwrite an existing glyph, delete that glyph first, and then create a new replacement. Leaving this checkbox unchecked is a safety measure so that you don't accidentally destroy some of your hard work. If you're making a two-glyph ligature, and you type in the names of two preexisting glyphs separated by an underscore, FontLab will show you the existing glyphs side by side as a preview of what you're about to create. Click OK.

4

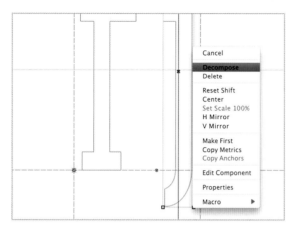

Your ligature glyph is now ready for you to edit. Find it in the font matrix in the main window.

5

Double click on its cell to open up the ligature in an editing window. You'll see that the two preexisting glyphs that will form your ligature are sitting there in gray. When a shape is grayed out in FontLab's editing window, it means that it's a live copy of a glyph—that is, in this example, at this point if you edit your font's "j," any changes you make will be reflected in the gray "j" in your ligature. If you're at an early stage of your font's development, you might want to keep these live copies of glyphs in your ligatures—if you're going to make substantial changes to your font, it's a waste of time to make the same change in a regular glyph and then in a ligature based on that glyph. But let's assume for this example that we're close to the end, and we want to make changes to the shapes that compose our ligature.

6

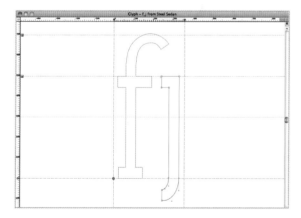

In the ligature's editing window, right-click on the gray live copy of the component you'd like to edit, and select Decompose. This unlinks the shape from its original glyph, and turns it into an editable shape in the ligature.

7

In this case, I've unlinked the "j" in the ligature from the regular "j" in the font, and made it editable. If you select the entire "j" shape, you can drag it closer to the "f." You can also delete the dot of the "j," and move the right sidebearing closer to the right edge of the "j." You've now got an "fj" ligature!

Continues…

8

The problem is that, even though you know it's an "fj" ligature, your font doesn't know this. To your font (and FontLab), you just created a brand new glyph with no special features besides being a glyph. You could just leave it this way, and hope that your font's users are savvy enough to find this glyph buried deep within your font. But there's no need to hide things from your users! This is where the magic of OpenType comes into play—with the proper instructions in your font, OpenType-aware programs will make automatic substitutions of your ligature wherever applicable.

9

To make the magic happen, make sure your OpenType panel is visible. Go to the Window menu, and choose Panels > OpenType. Next, click on the small + button in the lower left, and a new, blank OpenType feature is created for you.

10

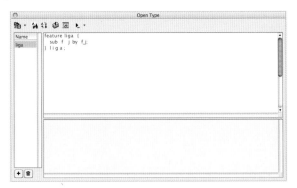

To change it to the feature you want (in this case, a ligature), click your mouse in the strings of "xxxx", delete these letters, and type in the OpenType feature you want: in this case, "liga", the OpenType feature name for ligatures. The name of the feature will automatically change in the left panel. Now in between the curly braces, type "sub f j by f_j;" which in plain English means "hey, OpenType-aware applications: if you spot the user typing in an 'f' and a 'j' adjacent to one another (in that order), replace those two glyphs with the one ligature 'fj'."

11

Here's what this ligature looks like in practice, compared to the two original glyphs side by side.

FINE POINTS

Currency symbols

There are dozens of currency symbols from around the world that you could include in your fonts. Of these, it is important to include at least the dollar ("$"), the cent ("¢"), the euro ("€"), the pound ("£"), the yen ("¥"), the florin ("ƒ"), and the generic currency symbol ("¤"). (This last symbol is meant to stand in as a generic symbol of any currency.)

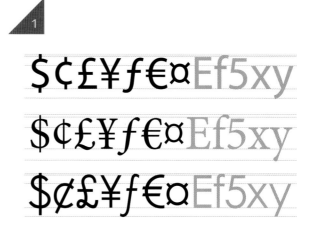

In many fonts, the currency symbols rise to slightly below the cap height, in keeping with the heights of these fonts' numeral glyphs. Note also that it's not unusual for the "S" part of the dollar signs to sit slightly above the baseline. In the fonts in image 1 (from top to bottom: Myriad Pro, Minion Pro, and Century Gothic), the first two harbor these quirks, while the third font treats its currency glyphs much more like traditional letters—the dollar, pound, yen, and euro are treated like normal capital letters, while the cent and florin are treated like lowercase letters.

In Century Gothic, there are small differences between glyphs you might expect to use the same components. Take the yen, for instance. In image 2 we have the same three fonts, and even though Century Gothic (bottom) treats its yen glyph like a "Y," note that the yen is marginally compressed at its top. (The "Y" is overlaid in magenta upon the yen, which is black.) This difference is more striking in Myriad Pro (top) and especially in Minion Pro (middle).

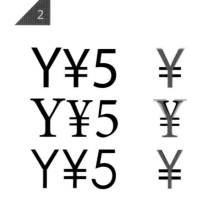

The same thing can be seen with the euro in image 3. It's generally not just a "C" with two horizontal strokes through its middle. The euro is often a compressed version of a "C." When it's not, as in Century Gothic (bottom), it is usually truncated. In fact, Century Gothic has it closer to "right" here, more so than Myriad Pro (top) and Minion Pro (middle)—the official specification of the euro design is pretty close to a truncated "O" with a vertical truncation on the bottom, and a continuous diagonal truncation of the top and the horizontal strokes.

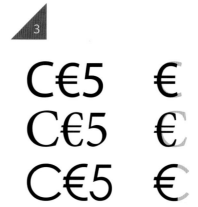

✳ ✳ ✳ *FontLab Tutorial*
CREATING DISCRETIONARY LIGATURES

The basic process for creating a discretionary ligature is the same as creating a standard ligature— there's just a small difference in the OpenType instructions.

As with the previous tutorial (see page 108), there are two basic steps: first, create the discretionary ligature glyph, then create the OpenType code in the font that tells other programs that this discretionary ligature is available to it. To work through the process, let's revisit the "id" discretionary ligature in the font Aeronaut, designed by Georg Herold-Wildfellner.

1

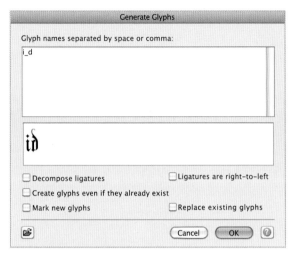

Go to the Glyph menu and choose "Generate Glyphs. Type "i_d" into the textbox and create the new ligature glyph.

2

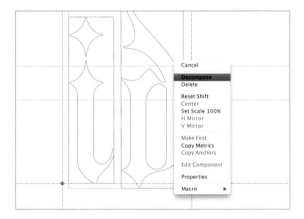

Open this new ligature glyph, then select both component shapes. Right-click on them, and select Decompose.

3

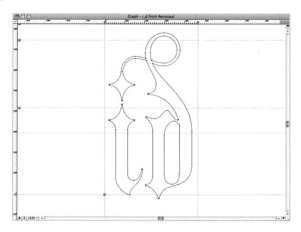

You then create the flourish by connecting the two shapes.

4

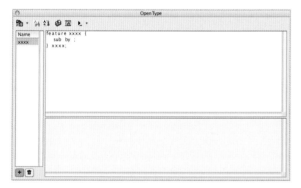

You then need to create the OpenType instructions to inform the font that it actually has a discretionary ligature available to it. Make sure the OpenType panel is visible by going to the Window menu, and choosing Panels > OpenType. Next, click on the small + button in the lower left, and a new, blank OpenType feature will be created.

5

To change it to the desired feature (in this case, a discretionary ligature), click in the strings of "xxxx," delete these letters, and type in "dlig",which is the OpenType feature name for discretionary ligatures. In between the curly braces, type "sub i d by i_d;" which in plain English means "hey, OpenType-aware applications: if the user has discretionary ligatures activated, and you spot the user typing in an 'i' and a 'd' adjacent to one another (in that order), replace those two glyphs with the one ligature 'id'."

6

Here's what this discretionary ligature looks like in practice, compared to the two original glyphs side by side.

✳✳✳ *FontLab Tutorial*
STYLISTIC ALTERNATES

It is fairly common practice for professional fonts to have some stylistic alternate glyphs available. These glyphs are alternatives to be used in special typographic circumstances. In image 1, the top set of letters uses Affair's standard glyphs; the bottom set uses Affair's stylistic alternates.

Stylistic alternates give your font's users the ability to have some interesting variety in how they set type. Look at the differences between the word "Zeno" with a standard "Z" versus the stylistic alternate in image 2.

Creating a stylistic alternate, as with ligatures, is a two-part process. First, create a new glyph and design it appropriately; second, use OpenType instructions to let the font know that it has stylistic alternates available to its users. Let's create a stylistic alternate glyph and apply the OpenType instructions.

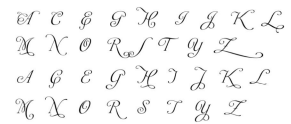

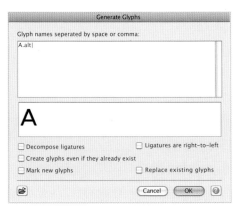

Make sure your font has an "A" glyph, then go to the Glyph menu and choose Generate Glyphs. In the text box, type in (without quotes) "A.alt". The ".alt" part is a convention that will make your life much easier in the long run. You definitely should use a dot after the glyph name; the "alt" suffix could be anything you like ("salt" would work too). If there's already an "A" glyph in your font, FontLab will show it in the preview window.

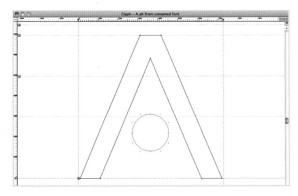

Find your new glyph in the main window, and double click on it to open it in an editing window. FontLab does not create a live copy of your original "A" for you to work with—it creates an editable, unlinked copy of your "A." Tweak your alternate "A" however you like (I've created a dot instead of a crossbar in mine).

3

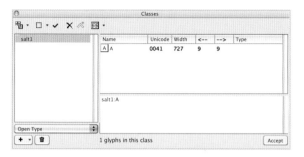

Open up the Classes panel (go to the Window menu and choose Panels > Classes), and click the plus sign in the lower left of the panel, and choose New OpenType Class. Select the text in the lower right of the panel, type "salt1:" there, and click on the "Accept" button. Now type "A" in the same space, after the colon. This tells FontLab you're creating a collection (or class) of glyphs called "salt1"

4

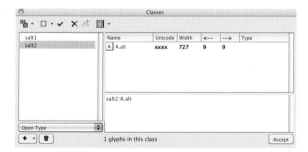

The idea is to create a class of original glyphs, and then create another class of alternate glyphs. Then we'll tell FontLab to substitute the alternates for the original, whenever a user of your font invokes the stylistic alternates property of your font in their page layout programs. Click on the plus sign again, and create another new OpenType class. Let's call this one "salt2". In this class, we'll put our A.alt glyph.

5

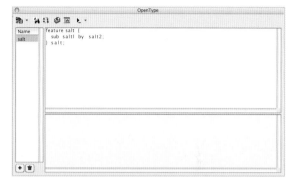

Now we have to provide instructions to make the font able to use stylistic alternates. Open the OpenType panel by going to the Window menu and choosing Panels > OpenType. Click on the plus sign to create a new OpenType feature template. The feature should read as follows: feature salt { sub @salt1 by @salt2; } salt; This tells the font and the programs that use it that there is a set of stylistic alternates available for use. If these are used, they should take glyphs that a user typesets (in the class "salt1") and substitute corresponding glyphs in another set (in the class salt2).

6

OpenType wants to know that this feature is enabled in your font, and you can tell it as much in the aalt instruction set ("aalt" stands for "Access All Alternates"). Click on the plus sign in the OpenType panel, and make sure the new feature created looks like this: feature aalt{ feature salt; } aalt; This acts like an early-warning system to the font that you're providing special instructions about an OpenType feature.

✳✳✳ *FontLab Tutorial*

SMALL CAPS

It used to be that you needed a completely separate font file for a font's small caps, but OpenType lets you embed small-cap glyphs in the same file as your normal glyphs, and also allows you to embed instructions for how those glyphs get used. The basic idea is this: you'll design your regular uppercase and lowercase glyphs, then you'll use your uppercase glyphs as a base from which to design a set of small-cap glyphs.

First, you'll need to create a lowercase "a" (along with an uppercase "A") so that you have a letter that will be substituted by your small cap "a." Open your font and double-click on the "a" cell in the main window to open it in an editing window.

To create a rudimentary "a," in case you need it, draw a circle, extending from just above the x-height line to just below the baseline. Then draw another circle, concentric to the first. Line them up properly, select both circles, then go to the Contour menu and select Transform > Delete Intersection. This gives you a disc shape.

These Are Not Small Caps

THESE ARE SMALL CAPS

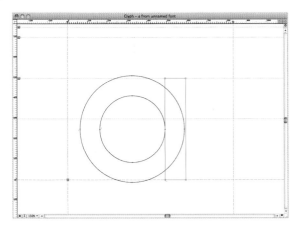

Now draw a rectangle near the right edge of the disc.

Select everything (cmd-A), then go to the Contour menu, and choose Transform > Merge Contours.

3

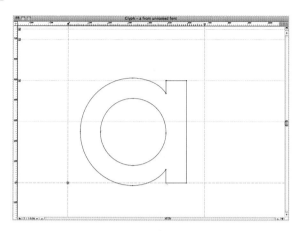

This merges all of the shapes into a whole.

4

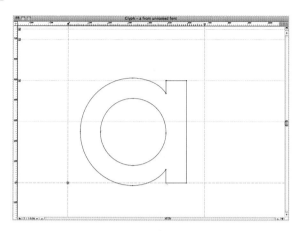

We can now create a small-cap "a" along with the appropriate OpenType instructions. First, we'll need to generate a new glyph. Go to the Glyph menu and select Generate Glyphs. Type (without quotes) "a.sc" in the text box. FontLab will assume that you're creating a glyph that has something to do with a lowercase "a," so the "a" appears in the preview box.

5

If you double click on the new glyph "a.sc" cell in the main window to open it in an editing window, you'll see that FontLab has provided you with a lowercase "a" as a starting point. Select all (cmd-A) and delete the a-shape. What we want is a small version of an uppercase "A." Go back to the main window, and double click on the "A" cell to open it in an editing window. Select all (cmd-A) and press cmd-C to copy the shape of the "A."

6

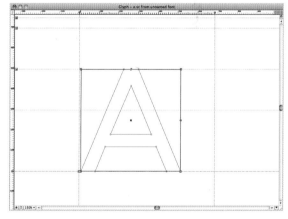

Get back to the main window, and double click on the "a.sc" cell to open it in an editing window. Press cmd-V to paste the A-shape into this glyph. Now select all (cmd-A) and double click on any edge of the A-shape to invoke the transform mode. While holding the Shift key, drag the upper-right corner of the transform box to make the entire shape smaller. The top of the shape should go to about the x-height of the glyph.

Continues...

7

Double click outside of the shape to deselect it and get it out of transform mode. We have made the small-cap glyph the right shape and the right height, but shrinking it uniformly has made the shape too thin—we want our small caps to be around the x-height of the font, but also to be close to the same thickness as the fully sized capital letters. To do this, select the whole glyph (cmd-A), then go to the Tools menu and select Actions.

9

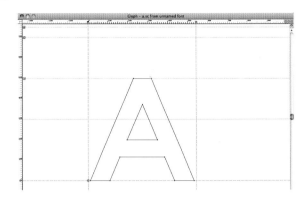

Click OK when you're ready, and FontLab thickens your small cap "a."

8

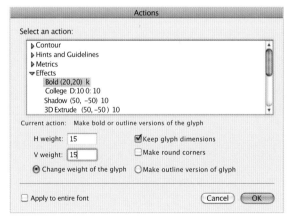

FontLab comes with a set of pre-scripted actions that you can use when designing your glyphs. In this case, we're going to use the Bold action. Click on the arrow next to "Effects" and click on the "Bold" action. The action has editable parameters; here, I've changed the two values to 15 instead of 20, to tone down the thickening that's about to happen.

10

Our next step is to do a little OpenType scripting. We're going to make a class for our lowercase glyphs, and a class for our small-cap glyphs that will be substituted for them in the proper circumstance. Then we'll instruct the font how to deal with these two classes the right way. So, first open up the Classes panel if it isn't already. (Window > Panels > Classes.) Now click on the plus sign in the lower left, and choose New OpenType Class.

11

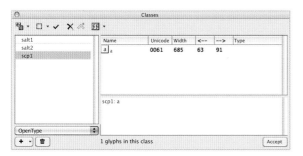

Name it "scp1" (type that before the colon in the lower-right pane, and make sure to click on Accept to make sure your change sticks). This name could be anything, but it's a good idea to name it something succinct and reminiscent of what the class is for. Now, after the colon in the lower-right pane, type "a" (without quotes), and click Accept again. This is your class of lowercase glyphs (there's only one so far, but you could add others as well—if you have more than one glyph in a class, just separate the glyph names with a space).

12

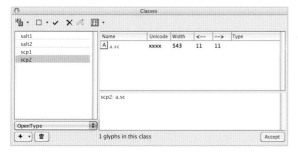

We need another class for our small caps. Click on the plus sign in the lower left of the Classes panel, and choose another New OpenType Class. Name this one scp2, following the same procedure as step 12. After the colon, add "a.sc" and click Accept.

13

Now we have the appropriate classes set up, but we need to tell OpenType what to do with them. Open the OpenType panel (Window > Panels > OpenType), and click on the plus sign in the lower-left pane to create a new OpenType feature. Rename the feature from its default "xxxx" to "smcp" (replace the "xxxx"s in the right pane). Now type "sub @scp1 by @scp2;13" in the body of the feature.

14

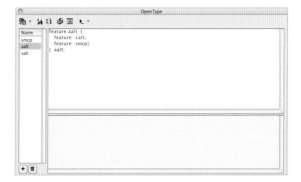

In plain English, this says, "whenever a user has the small-caps feature turned on in the program they're using, substitute the small-caps glyphs for the lowercase glyphs." In the OpenType panel, select the "aalt" feature (if your font doesn't have an "aalt" feature, click on the plus sign and rename that new feature "aalt"), and add the following bit of code: "feature smcp;". This tells the font that you have a small-cap feature that you want activated.

✳✳✳ *FontLab Tutorial*
SWASHES

Swash glyphs are decorative versions of their normal siblings, often used at the beginnings of words or paragraphs. The image below shows Sergiy Tkachenko's Bayadera 4F font; the top example is without swashes and the bottom example has swashes applied to the first and last letters, highlighted in green.

You can create a set of swash glyphs for your font and then include OpenType scripting to make them work in OpenType-aware applications. Let's step through the process of having one OpenType swash glyph in our font. Open the font you've been working with throughout this book, or create a new font altogether. (Alternatively, you could work on a preexisting font—just make sure to save the font as something else before you compile it.)

1

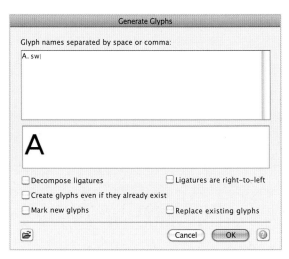

Make sure you have an "A" glyph. We'll be creating a swash "A" to complement it. Go to the Glyph menu and select Generate Glyphs. Type "A.sw" into the Glyph Names pane and click OK. The ".sw" suffix is arbitrary, but it will help us easily identify our swash glyphs throughout the next steps.

2

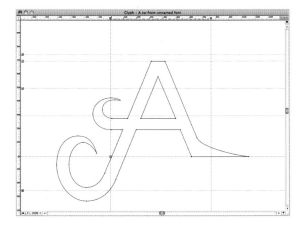

This creates a new glyph, based on your original "A," and ready for you to tweak. Here's an over-the-top one I created.

3

Font – Untitled [/Users/alec/Desktop/swash.vfb]

					breve	dotaccent		ring		hungarum	ogonek	caron	dotlessi										fraction	fi	fl	Lslash
---	---	---	---	---	˘	˙	---	◊	---	˝	˛	ˇ	ı	---	---	---	---	---	---	---	---	---	/	fi	fl	Ł

lslash	Zcaron	zcaron	space	exclam	quotedbl	numbers	dollar	percent	ampersa	quotesin	parenlef	parenri	asterisk	plus	comma	hyphen	period	slash	zero	one	two	three	four	five	six	seven	eight	nine
ł	Ž	ž		!	"	#	$	%	&	'	(	)	*	+	,	-	.	/	0	1	2	3	4	5	6	7	8	9

colon	semicol	less	equal	greater	question	at	A	B	C	D	E	F	G	H	I	J	K	L	M	N	O	P	Q	R	S	T	U	V
:	;	<	=	>	?	@	A	B	C	D	E	F	G	H	I	J	K	L	M	N	O	P	Q	R	S	T	U	V

W	X	Y	Z	bracket	backslas	bracketr	asciicir	undersc	grave	a	b	c	d	e	f	g	h	i	j	k	l	m	n	o	p	q	r	s
W	X	Y	Z	[	\	]	^	_	`	a	b	c	d	e	f	g	h	i	j	k	l	m	n	o	p	q	r	s

t	u	v	w	x	y	z	bracelef	bar	braceri	asciitild		Euro		quotesin	florin	quotedbl	ellipsis	dagger	daggerdb	circumf	perthous	Scaron	guilsingl	OE				
t	u	v	w	x	y	z	{	|	}	~		€		,	ƒ	„	…	†	‡	^	‰	Š	‹	Œ	---	---	---	---

quotelef	quoteri	quotedb	quotedbl	bullet	endash	emdash	tilde	tradema	scaron	guilsing	oe			Ydieres	uni00A0	exclamd	cent	sterling	currency	yen	brokenb	section	dieresis	copyrig	ordfemi	guillemo	logicaln	minus
'	'	"	"	•	–	—	˜	TM	š	›	œ	---	---	Ÿ		¡	¢	£	¤	¥	¦	§	¨	©	ª	«	¬	-

register	macron	degree	plusminu	twosupe	threesu	acute	mu	paragra	periodc	cedilla	onesupe	ordmasc	guillemo	onequar	onehalf	threequ	question	Agrave	Aacute	Acircum	Atilde	Adieres	Aring	AE	Ccedilla	Egrave	Eacute	Ecircum
®	¯	°	±	²	³	´	µ	¶	·	¸	¹	º	»	¼	½	¾	¿	À	Á	Â	Ã	Ä	Å	Æ	Ç	È	É	Ê

Edieresis	Igrave	Iacute	Icircum	Idieresis	Eth	Ntilde	Ograve	Oacute	Ocircum	Otilde	Odieresis	multiply	Oslash	Ugrave	Uacute	Ucircum	Udieres	Yacute	Thorn	germand	agrave	aacute	acircum	atilde	adieres	aring	ae	ccedill
Ë	Ì	Í	Î	Ï	Ð	Ñ	Ò	Ó	Ô	Õ	Ö	×	Ø	Ù	Ú	Û	Ü	Ý	Þ	ß	à	á	â	ã	ä	å	æ	ç

egrave	eacute	ecircum	edieres	igrave	iacute	icircum	idieresis	eth	ntilde	ograve	oacute	ocircum	otilde	odieres	divide	oslash	ugrave	uacute	ucircum	udieres	yacute	thorn	ydieres	A.alt	a.sc	l.sc	A.sw
è	é	ê	ë	ì	í	î	ï	ð	ñ	ò	ó	ô	õ	ö	÷	ø	ù	ú	û	ü	ý	þ	ÿ	A	A	L	𝒜

Size	Name	Names mode	Default Encoding	Glyph: A.sw [...]	Selected: 1 / 22

And here it is in the main screen's glyph matrix.

4

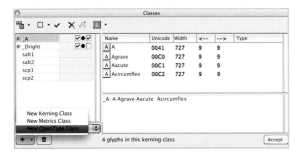

The next step is to create two OpenType classes—the first will be the container for all of our normal siblings that have swash versions of themselves, and the second will be the container for all of our swash glyphs. Go to the Window menu and select Panels > Classes.

5

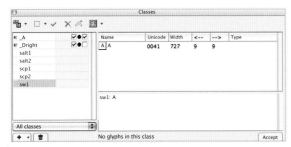

Click on the plus sign in the lower left of the Classes panel, and choose New OpenType Class. Change the name of the class in the lower right pane to "sw1" and type "A" after the colon. Then click the Accept button. This creates a class containing all of the glyphs that will have swash sibling glyphs related to them. (So far, we only have one such glyph. If there were others, you would include them in the lower right pane, after the colon.)

6

Create another new class to contain all of your swash glyphs. Repeat step 5, but use "sw2" and type "A.sw" after the colon. Click Accept when you're done.

7

We need a little OpenType magic to make our swash glyphs come to life in OpenType-aware applications. Open the OpenType panel by going to the Window menu and selecting Panels > OpenType. Next, click on the plus sign in the lower left of the panel to generate a new OpenType feature. Change the "xxxx"s to "swsh" and type "sub @sw1 by @sw2;" This tells OpenType-aware applications that whenever the OpenType swash feature is turned on, it should substitute any and all glyphs in the swash class for glyphs in the non-swash class.

8

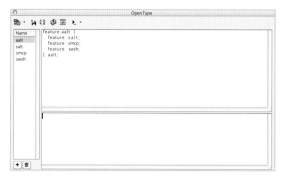

Get back to the OpenType panel, and click on the "AALT" feature in the left pane. (I'm assuming you already have an "AALT" feature set, from prior examples. If not, you'll have to add it.) Make sure that "swsh" is included in your list.

9

Now, when you compile your font and install it, you'll have a swash feature available in OpenType-aware layout programs.

FINE POINTS
The asterisk

The asterisk is one of those glyphs that's potentially more fun to design and talk about than it is to use in one's typography. It is not a particularly oft-used glyph—it is most used as shorthand to denote emphasis around a word ("*this* is important," for example) or as bullets for a list, simply, of course, because it occupies an easily reachable location on most computer keyboards. The real typographic uses for an asterisk are as a symbol denoting a footnote in a passage of text, as a placeholder to censor letters in a word or name, or as a divider between sections of text.

There is a huge variety in asterisks between fonts. In image 1, there are four asterisks from serif fonts in the left column (from top to bottom: Book Antiqua, Winthorpe, Minion Pro, Georgia), and four from sans serif fonts in the right (from top to bottom: Helvetica, Myriad Pro, Gill Sans, Futura). Every serif font I've seen has an asterisk that is very calligraphic (non-monoline) in nature. Most of their arms grow from skinny to fat as they go from the center outward. Minion Pro's is more of a traditional five-pointed star whose arms get skinnier as they go from center outward. In sans serif fonts, many asterisks are also calligraphic (in opposition from the rest of the glyphs in the font), but some are monoline, or close to it.

1

✳✳✳ *FontLab Tutorial*
CONTEXTUAL ALTERNATES

We've already seen the usefulness of stylistic alternates in OpenType fonts. There is another feature available to font creators who want to include alternate glyphs: contextual alternates.

Generally, stylistic alternates are meant to be wholesale substitutes—that is, if a book designer has a paragraph of text set in your font, and she turns on the stylistic alternates button in InDesign, every glyph for which you've provided a stylistic alternate will be replaced. Contextual alternates are used to substitute a glyph in a specific context. One such use is making symbol glyph substitutions; for example, when a user types in a hyphen followed by a greater-than symbol, you could have a contextual alternate that replaces that with a proper arrow symbol pointing to the right. Let's run through how to do that in a font.

2

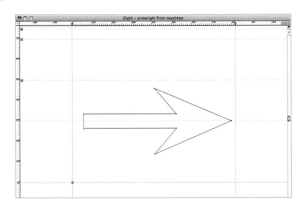

Now you need to design a right-arrow glyph. The Unicode specification includes just such a glyph—Unicode 2192, with the name "arrowright." Go to the Glyph menu and choose Generate Glyphs, type "arrowright" into the text box and click OK.

1

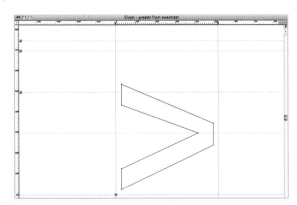

Open your font, making sure you've designed a hyphen and a greater-than glyph. The hyphen, obviously, is easy enough to design—usually it's a simple rectangle. The greater-than glyph has more variety in the ways it can be designed, but here's a pretty typical one. Generally, greater-than (and less-than) glyphs don't come to a point—their edges are all flat.

3

Design your right arrow however you see fit.

4

Do a little OpenType magic to make the desired substitution. Go to the Window menu, and choose Panels > OpenType. Now click on the plus sign in the lower left, and replace the "xxxx"s with "calt"s. The text is: feature calt { sub hyphen greater by arrowright; } calt; This is OpenType's way of saying "if you see a hyphen followed by a greater-than glyph, substitute an arrowright glyph in their place.

5

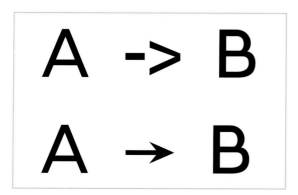

Above is a contextual alternate in practice as a hyphen and a greater than glyph are substituted by an arrow glyph.

GLYPH SUBSTITUTIONS

Another use for contextual alternates is making textual glyph substitutions based on context. For instance, say you have a font with the following glyphs: a swash "A," an "h," and a ligature glyph combining an "A" and an "h" in some unique and aesthetically interesting way. You could program your font, via OpenType instructions, to automatically replace any occurrence of the swash "A" followed by "h" with the "A-h" ligature. Here's the code you'd use to do it:

```
feature calt {
sub A.swsh h by Ah.alt2;
} calt;
```

The image below shows what it looks like in the Affair font. A swash "A" in front of an "h" is substituted by an alternate "A-h" ligature. The top shape in this image is two glyphs; the bottom shape is a single ligature.

Types of numerals

You are probably used to working with proportional lining numerals—"proportional" because they have varying widths, and "lining" because they all sit on the baseline and reach to the same height line (just shy of the font's cap height). Image 1 shows proportional lining figures in Minion Pro. The numerals are just slightly shorter than the capital letters.

Some fonts also come with a set of proportional oldstyle numerals. These have varying heights and sit at different vertical locations, mimicking varieties of lowercase letters. Image 2 shows proportional oldstyle figures in Minion Pro.

Some fonts also include tabular lining numerals. These take lining figures and create sidebearings around them that are all equal. This means that if you use them in a document (with kerning off) they will line up in perfect vertical columns, making them excellent for laying out tabular data. Image 3 shows lining figures in Minion Pro: proportional on the right; tabular on the left. Note how the tabular figures line up into neat columns.

The last type of numerals we'll explore are tabular oldstyle numerals. These take oldstyle numerals and create equal sidebearings around all of them, meaning that they will all align into perfect vertical columns. Image 4 shows oldstyle figures in Minion Pro: proportional on the right; tabular on the left. Note how the tabular figures line up into neat columns

✱✱✱ *FontLab Tutorial*

NUMERALS

Of course, OpenType gives you a great way to include these varieties of numerals in your fonts. First, you need to design all of these glyphs. Here's how to handle them in FontLab, once they're designed.

1

You should have consistent names for all of your numeral glyphs. Your normal (proportional lining figures) will be named what FontLab (and Unicode) wants you to name them: "zero," "one," "two," "three," "four," "five," "six," "seven," "eight," and "nine."

You will name your other glyphs as you create them (via the Glyph menu, choosing Generate Glyphs), and you should use consistent suffixes. For instance, you could name all of your proportional oldstyle glyphs: "zero.p_osf," "one.p_osf," "two.p_osf," "three.p_osf," "four.p_osf," "five.p_osf," "six.p_osf," "seven.p_osf," "eight.p_osf," and "nine.p_osf," where ".p_osf" stands for "proportional oldstyle figure."

Similarly, your tabular oldstyle glyphs could be named "zero.t_osf," "one.t_osf," "two.t_osf," "three.t_osf," "four.t_osf," "five.t_osf," "six.t_osf," "seven.t_osf," "eight.t_osf," and "nine.t_osf." Your tabular lining could be named "zero.tnum," "one.tnum," "two.tnum," "three.tnum," "four.tnum," "five.tnum," "six.tnum," "seven.tnum," "eight.tnum," and "nine.tnum."

The image below shows Museo Slab's glyphs in FontLab's main window. The standard numerals are highlighted above the other numerals—tabular lining numerals, proportional oldstyle, and tabular oldstyle.

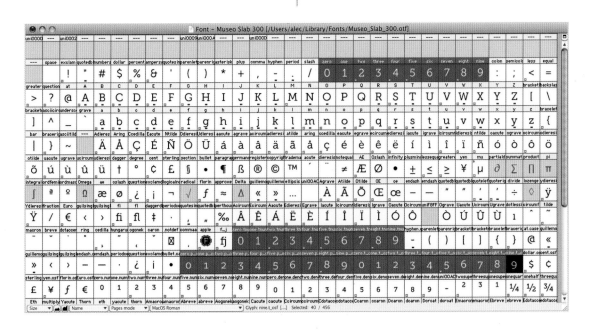

Continues…

2

Class Name	Type of Glyphs	Glyphs
lnum1	proportional oldstyle & tabular oldstyle	zero.p_osf, one.p_osf, two.p_osf, three.p_osf, four.p_osf, five.p_osf, six.p_osf, seven.p_osf, eight.p_osf, nine.p_osf, zero.t_osf, one.t_osf, two.t_osf, three.t_osf, four.t_osf, five.t_osf, six.t_osf, seven.t_osf, eight.t_osf, nine.t_osf
lnum2	proportional lining & tabular lining	zero, one, two, three, four, five, six, seven, eight, nine, zero.tnum, one.tnum, two.tnum, three.tnum, four.tnum, five.tnum, six.tnum, seven.tnum, eight.tnum, nine.tnum
onum1	proportional lining & tabular lining	zero, one, two, three, four, five, six, seven, eight, nine, zero.tnum, one.tnum, two.tnum, three.tnum, four.tnum, five.tnum, six.tnum, seven.tnum, eight.tnum, nine.tnum
onum2	proportional oldstyle & tabular oldstyle	zero.p_osf, one.p_osf, two.p_osf, three.p_osf, four.p_osf, five.p_osf, six.p_osf, seven.p_osf, eight.p_osf, nine.p_osf, zero.t_osf, one.t_osf, two.t_osf, three.t_osf, four.t_osf, five.t_osf, six.t_osf, seven.t_osf, eight.t_osf, nine.t_osf
pnum1	tabular lining & tabular oldstyle	zero.tnum, one.tnum, two.tnum, three.tnum, four.tnum, five.tnum, six.tnum, seven.tnum, eight.tnum, nine.tnum, zero.t_osf, one.t_osf, two.t_osf, three.t_osf, four.t_osf, five.t_osf, six.t_osf, seven.t_osf, eight.t_osf, nine.t_osf
pnum2	proportional lining & proportional oldstyle	zero one two three four five six seven eight nine zero.p_osf one.p_osf two.p_osf three.p_osf four.p_osf five.p_osf six.p_osf seven.p_osf eight.p_osf nine.p_osf

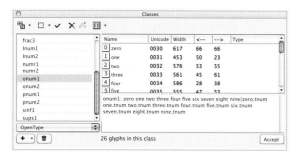

Once the naming is done, the next step is to set up some OpenType classes. Go to the Window menu and select Panels > Classes. Click on the plus sign in the lower left of the panel and select New OpenType class. I'll follow the naming conventions that Jos Buivenga used for his Museo Slab family, and I'll be showing screenshots of his font in FontLab throughout the following examples. (The class names are arbitrary—feel free to name them whatever you want.) The table above includes the classes we'll be using, and the glyphs those classes will contain:

3

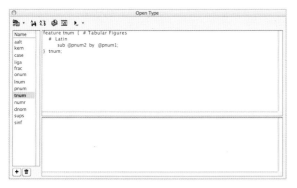

4

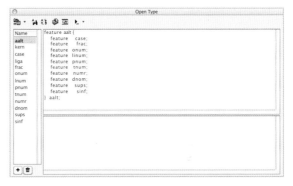

Now we have to set up some code to make the OpenType magic happen. You know how to create OpenType features by now. Make sure the OpenType panel is showing (Window > Panels > OpenType), and click on the plus sign in the lower left of the panel. Here are the four features we want to add:

feature lnum { sub @lnum1 by @lnum2; } lnum;
feature onum { sub @onum1 by @onum2; } onum;
feature pnum { sub @pnum1 by @pnum2; } pnum;
feature tnum { sub @pnum2 by @pnum1; } tnum;

The screenshot above shows Museo Slab's tnumOpenType feature in FontLab's OpenType panel. "lnum" stands for "lining numerals," "onum" for "oldstyle numerals," "pnum" for "proportional numerals," and "tnum" for "tabular numerals." In our lnumfeature, we're telling OpenType to substitute the lnum2class for the lnum1class, which means substituting our combined proportional lining & tabular lining glyphs (lnum1) for our combined proportional oldstyle & tabular oldstyle glyphs (lnum2) wherever they occur. A simpler translation is: substitute lining glyphs for oldstyle glyphs.

The same interpretation holds for the other three features we've added. The onumfeature tells OpenType to substitute oldstyle glyphs for lining glyphs. The pnumfeature says substitute proportional glyphs for tabular glyphs. And the tnumfeature says just the opposite of the pnum feature: substitute tabular glyphs for proportional glyphs.

Go to the OpenType panel and add these new features to the aaltfeature that should already exist, if you're using the font you've been using for other examples in this book. Here's what Museo Slab's OpenType features panel looks like. Note lnum, onum, pnum, and tnumfeatures referenced in the aaltfeature.

OTHER OPENTYPE FEATURES

There are many other OpenType features that you can include in your fonts. Here are a few others to whet your appetite.

Feature	OpenType feature name
Superscript	sups
Subscript	subs
Contextual swash	cswh
Contextual ligatures	clig
Fractions	frac
Numerator	numr
Denominator	dnom
Ornaments	ornm
Stylistic sets	ss01 - ss20
Historical forms	hist
Terminal form	fina
Initial forms	init

Hinting

For all the wondrousness of vectors, and how they scale without degradation or corruption to any size, large or small, we live in an imperfect, vector-free reality. Our output devices—monitors and printers—are raster devices. That is, they display things via the turning off and on (and coloring and intensifying/mellowing) of small dots. The dots that compose our monitors are called pixels. Even with ever-decreasing pixel sizes, ever-increasing numbers of pixels on our displays, and technological display advances, we still must deal with the fact that raster technology degrades and corrupts the beautiful vectors that compose our fonts.

Why does this happen? The pixels that compose our screens are arranged in a grid; and no matter how fine that grid is, each pixel in that grid can only be on or off. This means that there can be no perfectly straight diagonal lines on the screen. Take Helvetica's "N" as an example (image 1). If we overlay a grid on top of it, we see that the diagonal of the "N" crosses boxes in the grid without fully covering them. But this cannot be translated by a computer monitor, because each box in the grid (each pixel) must be either entirely on or entirely off. So to display this "N" on screen, our first option is to completely fill each box that the diagonal crosses. As you can see, this makes for an ugly "N" with a diagonal that is entirely too thick. One other choice is to selectively highlight some pixels that the diagonal crosses. It's still a bit crooked, but is a far more attractive glyph than the first "N" we just digitized.

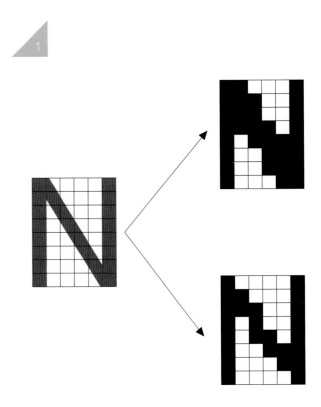

✳ ✳ ✻ *FontLab Tutorial*
AUTOHINTING IN FONTLAB

One solution to this problem is hinting—the specifying of instructions to the font about how to treat each glyph at small sizes on raster displays. Hinting is a Byzantine art which we'll just scratch the surface of here. Thankfully, FontLab comes equipped with an autohinting feature that works pretty well and is good enough for most purposes. Let's explore how to apply it.

2

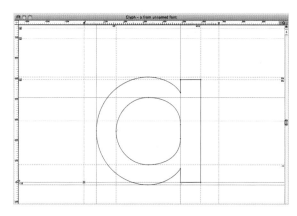

When the glyph is autohinted, FontLab will display a series of green-and-black dashed and solid lines in the glyph's editing window.

1

To autohint a single glyph, select it in the main window, then go to the Tools menu and choose Hints & Guides > Autohinting.

3

If you want to autohint your entire font in one fell swoop, select all your glyphs (cmd-A in the main window), go to the Tools menu, and choose Hints & Guides > Autohinting. If the green-and-black hinting lines are displayed in a glyph's editing window, and there is either nothing or a green H in the lower-left corner of the glyph's cell in the main window, your glyph is properly autohinted. However, at this point we have to talk about a FontLab autohinting quirk that surfaces from time to time: the dreaded red H. If you've autohinted a glyph that FontLab has problems with, FontLab applies hinting instructions that almost work, then displays a red H in the lower-left corner of the glyph's cell in the main window.

Continues…

4

If you try to compile a font with one or more glyphs with this red H displayed, you will get error messages, and the compilation will potentially fail. Short of manual hinting, fixing this problem is unfortunately a matter of trial and error in the editing window (there seems to be no science to it, as far as I can tell), and occasionally frustration will tempt you to simply remove all hinting from the offending glyph. (To unhint a glyph, select it in the main window, go to the Tools menu, and choose Hints & Guides > Remove Hints > Both.) But there are a few strategies you can try in order to fix the problems autohinting has wrought.

6

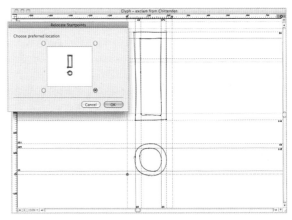

To relocate startpoints in a glyph, first remove existing hints from the glyphs (go to the Tools menu and choose Hints & Guides > Remove Hints > Both), and then go to the Contour menu and select Paths > Relocate Startpoints. A new screen appears, where you can change each of the glyph's startpoints from one node to another. After relocating the startpoints of your glyph, autohint it again and see if the red H comes back. Sometimes these changes make the red H disappear, and your font will compile fine.

5

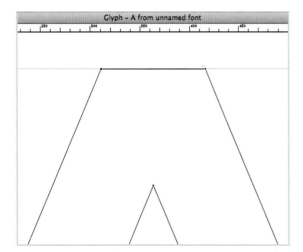

The first strategy is to relocate the startpoints. A startpoint is the node at which a contour of the glyph begins being drawn, and is notated in the FontLab editing window with a small gray arrow.

7

The second strategy involves nodes at extremes. If your troublesome glyph doesn't have nodes at its extremes—that is, nodes at the outermost and innermost points of its contours—this could prevent your glyph from being hinted correctly. To fix this problem, first remove hints from your glyph, and then go to the Contour menu and select Nodes at Extremes. Now autohint the glyph again to see if the red H comes back.

8

If the first two strategies don't help, you may have only three options left. You could wade into manual hinting; you could start moving nodes around in the glyph; or you could give up and remove all hints from the glyph entirely. If you find the proper node to move, sometimes all it will take is a one-unit nudge to get the autohinting to work for you. But if you're completely satisfied with how your glyph is composed, a one-unit nudge might offend your sensibilities. So you have to decide which is the lesser of two evils: no hinting for one of your glyphs, or hinting the glyph at the cost of altering the glyph slightly. If you try moving nodes around, remember to remove hints from the glyph, move a node one unit, and then try autohinting the glyph again.

MANUAL HINTING

A usual culprit in the problem of the red H is that standard (Type 1) hinting requires that hints do not overlap each other. Let's look at the case of a "B" glyph and how hinting plays out for it. What FontLab would love is if the two lobes of your "B" were exactly the same size. That way, it could have only one vertical hint running from top to bottom, covering both lobes (image 1).

Unfortunately, most "B"s are not so cooperative, and have their bottom lobes bigger than their top (images 2 and 3). There are two vertical hints—one covering the width of the top lobe, and one covering the width of the bottom. These overlap, which is a problem for standard hinting (image 4).

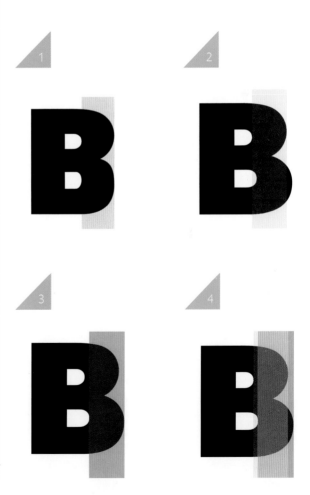

✱✱✱ *FontLab Tutorial*
MANUAL HINT REPLACEMENT

The solution to the overlapping problem is to give special instructions to hints to limit how far they extend vertically. This is called hint replacement. To bring this back around to our hinting issues above: our happy green H in cells of the main window means hint replacement is on and is working. Our unhappy red H means hint replacement is on but not working (there are overlapping hints there). If there's no H, it means that there's no hint replacement in the glyph. So let's step through the process of manually hinting a "B."

2

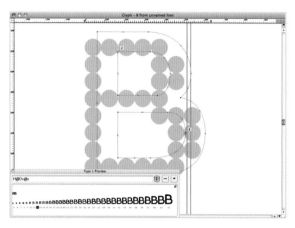

Now we can start creating hints. To create a vertical hint, move your cursor into the left-hand ruler, hold the Command key (Control on a PC) and drag from left to right. (If you don't hold the Command/Control key while doing this, you will be creating a guide instead of a hint. A guide has only one line, while a hint has two.) A thin strip will follow your cursor—drop it so that the right side of the strip aligns with the rightmost point of the upper lobe of the "B."

1

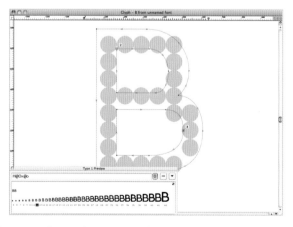

Open your font and create a simple sans serif "B." Remove any hinting (Tools > Hints & Guides > Remove Hints > Both), then open up the Type 1 Hinting editor by going to the Tools menu and choosing Hints & Guides > Type 1 Hinting.

3

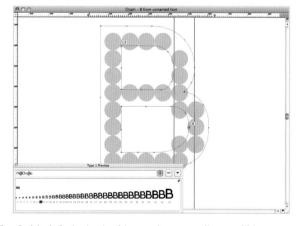

FontLab's default size in this case is too small, so we'll have to expand it. Hold the Shift key and drag the left side of the hint so it aligns with the inner node of the top lobe. Each change you make in the hinting is reflected in the preview pane.

4

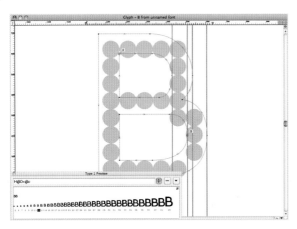

Now let's make another vertical hint for the bottom lobe. Hold the Command/Control key and drag from the left ruler to the right, aligning the rightmost side of the new hint with the rightmost node of the bottom lobe. Again, we have to resize it to cover the width of the bottom lobe. Hold the Shift key and drag the left side of the hint to align with the inner node of the bottom loop. The overlap of the two vertical hints is now highlighted by FontLab in orange.

6

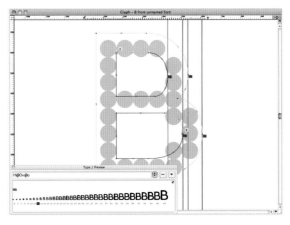

Do the same for the innermost node of the bottom lobe, as well as for the outermost and innermost nodes of the top lobe. After replacement points have been specified, our glyph is now properly hinted, as far as dealing with overlapping hints. The H in the upper right of the editing window should turn green, signifying that your hinting replacement is active and working correctly.

5

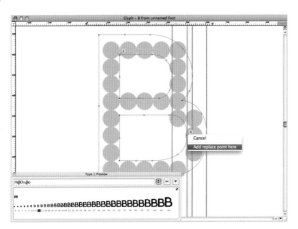

Now we have to specify replacement points—points at which the magic of hint replacement take place. Right-click on the outermost node of the bottom lobe, and select Add Replace Point Here.

7

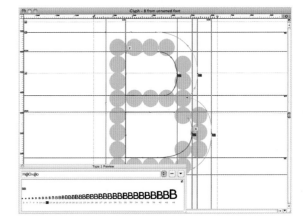

Add a vertical hint for the left stem and horizontal hints for the top, middle, and bottom bars of the "B." To create a horizontal glyph, hold Command/Control while dragging down from inside the top ruler bar.

Compiling your font

Before compiling your font, turn on the Audit layer and think about fixing problems it shows with each glyph. I say "think about" it because fixing problems shown by the Audit layer can make minor changes to the contours of your glyphs. There are excellent fonts out there that will show "problems" with the Audit layer, but are actually fine. For instance, below is Adobe Caslon Pro's "M" with the Audit layer turned on. Notice the small red arrows around the glyph's contours. These are points at which FontLab's Audit layer thinks problems exist.

Let's step through the process of auditing/fixing glyphs using the O-E ligature from the font Tingle.

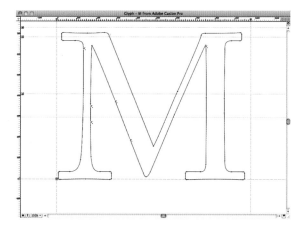

✳✳✳ *FontLab Tutorial*
THE FONT AUDIT LAYER

1

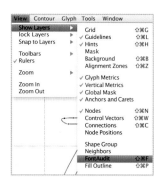

You can show the Audit layer by going to View menu, and choosing Show Layers > FontAudit.

2

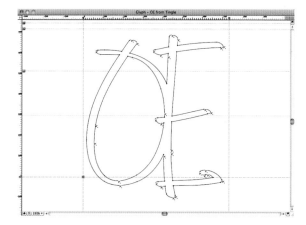

If FontLab thinks there are problems with a glyph, it will mark them with small red arrows in the editing window. Here's the same glyph with the Audit layer turned on. FontLab thinks that there are a lot of problems here; I've used this font in print jobs, and I've never had any problems with it.

3

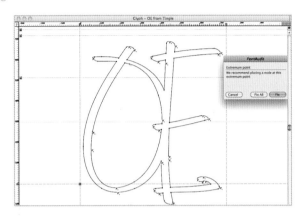

To fix a problem, single-click on one of the red arrows, and select Fix from the dialog box.

5

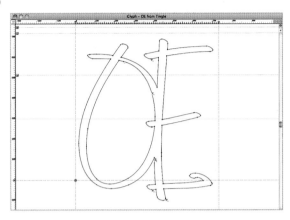

If you have several Audit layer problems to fix, click on one of them and choose Fix All from the dialog box. However, fixing one problem can generate a new one.

4

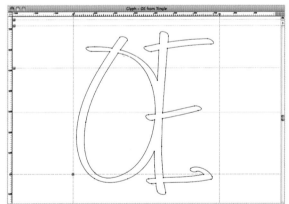

This is usually a destructive operation—that is, it will fix the problem but may (hopefully, and usually, minimally) change the appearance of your glyph. Pay close attention to the before and after of each fix you let FontLab administer, and make sure you're happy with the result. It's better (usually) to live with one of FontLab's red arrows than to see your glyphs changed against your better judgement.

6

Although FontLab usually makes headway through the audit problems if you keep clicking on Fix All again and again, the program can get into an infinite loop of swapping one problem for another and never stopping. If you find this happening after a few rounds of clicking Fix All, you can either leave one problem there and be done with it, or you can start tweaking nodes. Sometimes, all it takes is a one-unit nudge to fix a problem in the Audit layer. Of course, a one-unit nudge, though small, means you are slightly changing the shape of your glyph to accommodate a solution that FontLab thinks is necessary. In the battle between fixing little red arrows and keeping your aesthetic integrity, aesthetic integrity should generally win.

Keep in mind that fixing problems in the Audit layer can impact on your hinting. If you correct audit problems at this stage, you should unhint and re-hint any glyphs that you've fixed.

Once you've fixed all of the problems you think you should, and re-hinted your font where needed, you're ready to compile your font into a usable format. Before you do this, step through the Font Info window.

✳ ✳ ✳ *FontLab Tutorial*
THE FONT INFO WINDOW

In order to make your font compilation go smoothly, you'll need to go through all of the screens of the Font Info window. FontLab makes the process as easy as possible—if you ever see a little green diamond next to a text box or set of text boxes, click on it to have FontLab figure out what information should go there. To get to the Font Info window, click on the File menu and choose Font Info.

FONT NAMES

Naming your font requires a little research on your part to make sure the name isn't already being used by someone else. Check the major reseller sites first—MyFonts.com and Fonts.com—and then check Google. It helps, of course, if you're naming your font something obscure or invented—you're less likely to have a naming conflict over a font named "Grphrudlphum" than one named "Happy." (Yes, Happy is actually a font family.)

1

Enter your font's name in the Family Name text box. (It's "family name" instead of "font name" because your font name will be something like "Grphrudlphum Regular" or "Grphrudlphum Bold", where "Grphrudlphum" is the family name and "Regular" and "Bold" are style names.)

Next, choose the font's weight. FontLab provides you with a list of choices—ultralight, thin, extralight, light, book, regular, normal, medium, demibold, semibold, bold, extrabold, heavy, black, ultra, ultrablack, fat, and extrablack. You'll notice that if you change this, the numeric text box to the right changes its value as well. These numbers correspond to standard values used to denominate font weights: 100, 300, 500, 700, and 900; and correspond to thin, light, medium, bold, and black. If the font is bold and/or italic, check the corresponding checkbox to the right.

2

Choose your font's width. FontLab's list of choices are ultra-condensed, extra-condensed, condensed, semi-condensed, medium, semi-expanded, expanded, extra-expanded, and ultra-expanded. Again, these are standard monikers.

3

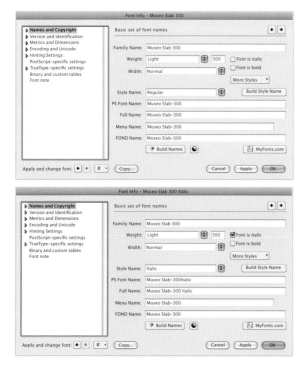

Now choose the style name. FontLab's list of choices is limited to regular, italic, bold, and bold italic. If you have a font that's, say, light—in other words, isn't regular, italic, bold, or bold italic—then you might be at a loss as to what to choose here. The screenshots above show what Jos Buivenga, creator of the renowned Museo font families, has done with his Museo Slab 300. Even though Museo Slab 300 is a light font, he has named its style "Regular," and then filled in the other names accordingly.

Once you've filled in the family name, the weight, the width, and the style name, you can let FontLab generate the appropriate names beneath the style name, simply by clicking on the button with the green diamond that also says Build Names.

4

Click on the arrow next to the Names and Copyright label on the left to expand the subnav, and you'll see you're not even close to finished with your font's naming and other related details. You can let FontLab do the work for you here and click on the button labeled Build OpenType Names.

5

The Additional OpenType names screen is rarified territory that font creators rarely step into. I've seen talk of the information from hardcore font nerds and Python programmers, but unless you learn otherwise from a wise source, you should probably leave all of these fields blank.

6

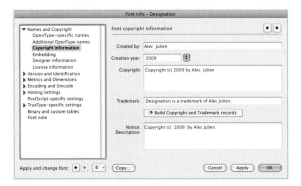

In the copyright information section, enter your name and the year, and click on the green diamond button to fill in the rest of the fields. You can edit them to your liking.

7

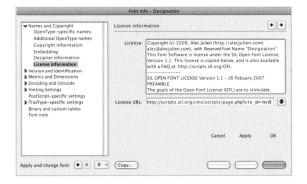

You can choose to have more restrictions on your font in the Embedding settings pull-down list. For instance, if you choose "Embedding of this font is not allowed," then anyone who uses your font in, say Adobe Illustrator, will have major problems saving documents with your font included in it. Unless you have a very good reason to not allow font embedding, I recommend giving your font's users as much latitude as you can. Don't treat your customers like criminals.

8

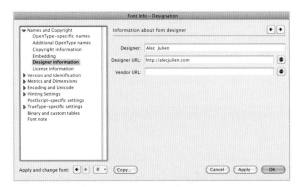

The Designer Information screen is pretty self-explanatory. Enter your name (assuming you designed this font) and your URL. If your font is exclusively sold by one distributor, you can enter that URL here as well.

9

If you have a license for your font (and you should), you can enter it here. Alternatively (or in addition), you could put a URL to your license information here.

✳✱ FontLab Tutorial
VERSION AND IDENTIFICATION

If you think you're new to versioning, well, you're probably not really new to it. Remember the last time you updated, say, Firefox, and it told you that you were downloading version 8.0.1? Well, that's versioning at work. The general idea is this: the first number is the major release version, and any numbers following it are minor version updates. So Firefox 8.01 means that the company has had 8 major versions of the software, and then one minor update to the 8th major version.

I've rarely seen a font that has been tweaked more than a handful of times in its lifetime. Generally, you may find a few bugs in your font that you'll fix over the course of one or two updates. In that case, you might release your first version as 1.0, and then update to 1.001 or 1.01 or 1.1, depending on how major your fixes are. Another update later down the road might be 1.002 or 1.02 or 1.2. If you release a drastically updated, significantly changed version of your font, you should think about calling the new version 2.0.

Beware of changing your fonts too dramatically. Your users might be using your original version in a great many documents, and if they update your font, their documents might also become updated, and with unexpected changes. If you make a dramatic change like this, at least make sure to include a note in the font's package that alerts the user to the change.

1

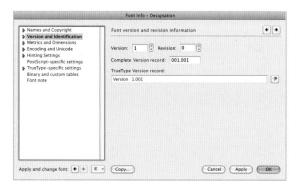

Click on the Version and Identification label on the left of the font info window, and you'll be brought to a whole new section of information to be filled out. In the initial view, you are asked to detail the version information of your font. Fill out the information as you see fit, and your font will be tagged with the version number.

2

Click on the green arrow next to the Version and Identification label on the left to expand the subnav, then click on the Identification settings.

Continues...

3

Assuming you've filled out all of the other information preceding this, you can just click on the little green diamond to autofill the TrueType Unique ID record. Don't worry about the Type 1 ID numbers. For the TrueType vendor code, you can leave it blank until you do the legwork of getting a code from Microsoft. You can go to http://www.microsoft.com/typography/links/vendorlist.aspx and follow the instructions to try to get your unique code; or don't bother—it's not a huge deal, but can potentially help your foundry's name show up in other websites and applications. It can't hurt to have a link to your website on Microsoft's site, in any event. Now update the creation date of your font if necessary, and you're done with this screen.

4

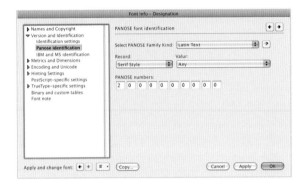

The Panose identification screen is something you can safely ignore. However, if you're interested in the subject, the idea is that the string of numbers in the Panose numbers field is supposed to help identify characteristics of your font by detailing them one at a time via a preset code.

5

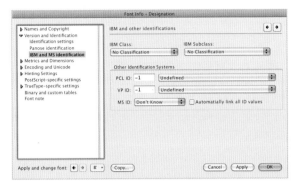

Again, the IBM screen is something you can safely ignore. Quite frankly, I'm not even sure what archaic holdover this information is all about, but I wouldn't be surprised if it disappears from future versions of FontLab.

✳ ✳ ✳ *FontLab Tutorial*
METRICS AND DIMENSIONS

The next stage in compiling your font is to complete the information on metrics and dimensions.

1

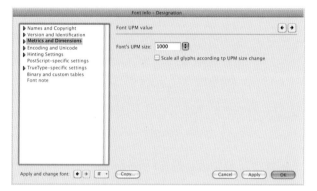

Your first screen is about UPM size. UPM stands for "Units Per M," "M" being short for "Em,",which is confusing because generally an em is supposed to characterize the approximate width of a lowercase "m" (as in "em dash"). But that's not what "Em" means here. According to the FontLab documentation, "Em" means "the size of the grid on which all glyph coordinates are defined," which basically means your UPM dictates how fine a grid you're working with in FontLab. Most of my examples in this book have been based on a UPM of 1,000 (FontLab's default). With UPM equal to 1,000, your x-height might be in the 500 region, and your cap height in the 700 region. Bumping nodes around one unit at a time is thus dependent on how big your units are, which is dependent on your font's UPM. Unless you need to have much finer-grained control over your nodes, a UPM of 1,000 is generally fine. (According to folklore around the Internet, UPM is supposed to equal your ascender height plus your descender absolute value.)

2

In the Key Dimensions screen, you can ignore the Set the Dimensions For The Master pull-down list. This refers to the incredibly arcane subject of multiple master fonts, which falls well beyond the scope of this book. (The basic idea behind a multiple master font is that it makes it easier to develop multiple weights of a font family. But "easier" here is very difficult to quantify, since the learning curve for mastering multiple master technology is very steep.) I've heard rumors that multiple master fonts are a dying breed, so you can ignore the subject if you wish.

3

If you've designed your font consistently, the next few fields will be easy for FontLab to auto-generate when you click the green diamond. FontLab is pretty good at sniffing out the basic vertical metrics of fonts. However, you might have an issue with a font that has, say, glyphs with different descenders. As a general rule of thumb, you want to make the descender value here the biggest descender of any of your glyphs, and FontLab might not choose the biggest one for you. If you choose a descender value that's not large enough, your largest descending glyph will overlap the tops of your other glyphs a line below it in page-layout software and word-processing programs.

Continues...

4

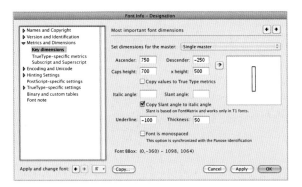

If your font is italic, FontLab should be able to detect it. However, I have had instances where FontLab thinks my font is slanted at 12°, when it's really 11°, so you should double check what FontLab fills in for you.

5

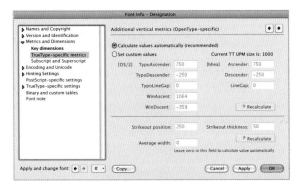

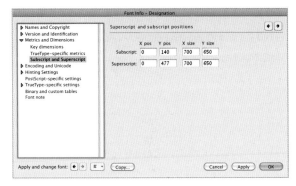

For the next two sections, you should almost always let FontLab do the calculating of values for you. There is an infamous problem that very occasionally crops up when your ascender and descender don't sum to your UPM value, but you can fix this in the True Type-specific metrics screen if need be.

✳✳✳ *FontLab Tutorial*
ENCODING AND UNICODE

Microsoft tells us that a codepage is "a list of selected character codes in a certain order. Codepages are usually defined to support specific languages or groups of languages that share common writing systems. For example, codepage 1253 provides character codes required in the Greek writing system."

In the past, an operating system or application could change the behavior of a keyboard by changing a font's codepage from one language to another. In one instance, a font's user could be typing a document in English; then, by switching codepages, the same font could produce Cyrillic output. Now, we have Unicode, the standard developed to represent/encode letters of alphabets,which can encode millions of glyphs within a single font. This standard, together with Unicode-ready fonts and applications that can take advantage of this technology, means that codepages are an outdated scheme. However, it's best to specify this information in FontLab, just to be on the safe side.

2

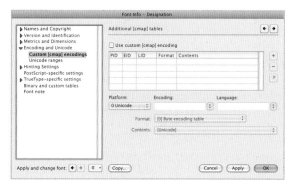

The Custom [cmap] encodings screen is one of those for-hardcore-nerds-only screens in FontLab. The acronym "cmap" is short for "Character To Glyph Index Mapping Table" and refers to a table of information inside an OpenType font. According to Microsoft: "This 'cmap' encoding is not required. It provides a compatibility mechanism for non-Unicode applications that use the font as if it were Windows ANSI encoded."

1

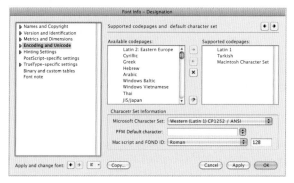

The initial Encoding and Unicode screen is the way TrueType and OpenType fonts communicate to the operating system what codepages are available from them to the OSs. FontLab does a good job of calculating these choices for you, if you simply click on the green diamond.

3

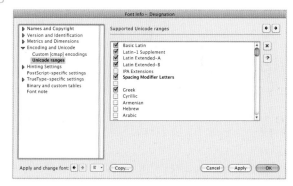

The Unicode ranges screen is where you can detail for your modern, Unicode-aware, OpenType font which Unicode ranges are included in your font—that is, which Unicode ranges have glyphs in them in your font. Click on the green diamond to let FontLab do the hard work of figuring this out for you.

✳ ✳ ✺ *FontLab Tutorial*

HINTING SETTINGS

Next up is the Hinting Settings section. If you've been good about setting up your hinting, and about setting consistent vertical metrics throughout your font (ascender, descender, cap height, and x-height), then this section should be a breeze.

2

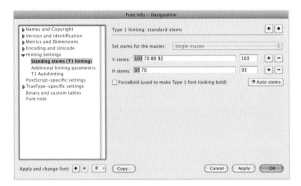

In the Standard stems (T1 hinting) screen, you should again just be able to click on the green diamond to have FontLab fill in all of the right information for you.

1

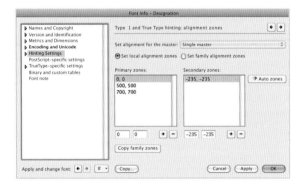

Simply click on the green diamond to automatically fill in the right values.

3

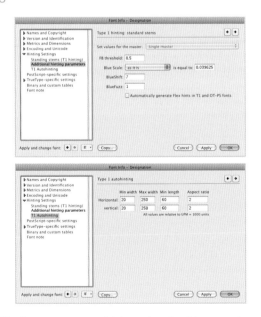

The last two screens of this section should not need any adjusting whatsoever.

✳ ✳ ✳ *FontLab Tutorial*

POSTSCRIPT-SPECIFIC AND TRUETYPE-SPECIFIC SETTINGS

This should also be a quick section to get through as FontLab can do a lot of the work for you.

2

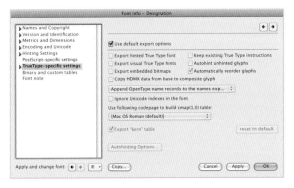

In the initial screen for TrueType-specific settings, you shouldn't have to change anything. If you're compiling a TrueType version of your font, and for some reason the default export options aren't suitable, you could change them here.

1

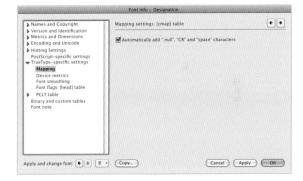

In the one and only screen for PostScript-specific settings, you shouldn't have to change anything. If you're compiling a PostScript version of your font, and for some reason the default export options aren't suitable, you could change them here.

3

In the Mapping screen, you can have FontLab automatically generate a couple of special characters that you might not otherwise think to include: the null character, a carriage return character, and a space character. It's generally a good idea to check off this box.

Continues…

4

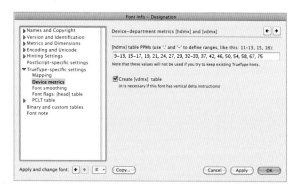

FontLab does the number crunching for you in the Device metrics screen. The following screens, Font smoothing and Font flags: [head] table, also require no input from you.

5

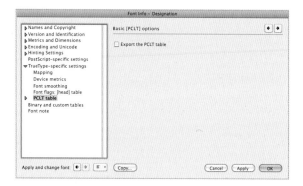

We have another full set of submenu items under the PCLT menu. The PCLT screen itself is not very daunting. Just keep the checkbox there unchecked and you're good to go on to the next screen.

6

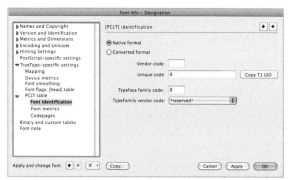

The only info on the Font Identification screen you'll need is Native Format. Let FontLab do the rest of the work.

7

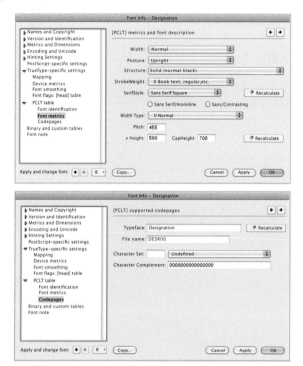

The next screens—Font Metrics and Codepages—need some attention. Thankfully, the green diamonds will do an excellent job of parsing your font and returning the right values in the right fields. You will not need to manipulate the final two sections— Binary and custom tables and Font note.

✳ ✳✳ *FontLab Tutorial*
COMPILING YOUR FONT

Now you're finally ready to compile your font!

1

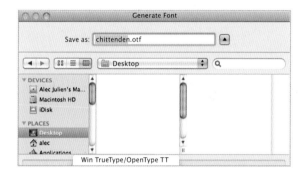

Close the Font Info window, and go to the File menu and choose "Generate Font…" A dialog box appears where you can name your font and choose the sort of font you'd like to compile.

2

Some designers generate their font in each of several formats, and bundle them for sale together. In case any of your clients need a particular format, this approach will obviously make everyone happy. I personally just generate one format; for all of my recent fonts I have used OpenType PS (a file with the extension .otf). For one thing, most of my recent fonts incorporate OpenType features that would be lost in Type 1 and non-OpenType TrueType formats. For another thing, I edit all of my fonts using PostScript curves and with PS direction. So it's a natural thing to compile to OpenType PS.

Creating a font family

Once you've created a font, you might want to start thinking about expanding it into a family. Thanks to Windows and word-processing software, regular, italic, bold, and bold italic are the general basis for a family—for a non-handwriting, non-script typeface, that is. Your font's users might very well not be sophisticated designers, but people using Microsoft Word, and wanting to press cmd-I and cmd-B to their hearts' contents. So you should consider providing them with these options.

ITALICS AND OBLIQUES

We addressed some basics of slanted letterforms on page 19, but here's a brief refresher. Italic fonts are generally slanted at around 12° to the right from their regular siblings. Oblique fonts are similarly slanted. What distinguishes an italic font from an oblique font is that the italic version is generally not only slanted, but flourished or otherwise artistically changed as well.

In image 1, the top example shows Frutiger and Frutiger Italic. The italic version is really a pure oblique—the glyphs have been slanted but not at all changed aside from the angle. The middle example shows Myriad Pro and Myriad Pro Italic. The italics here are somewhere in between obliques and italics— for instance, the "a," "b," "e," and "q" have changed significantly besides being slanted, but the "i," "l," "r," and "u" have just been slanted, not flourished in any way. The bottom example shows Minion Pro and Minion Pro Italic. Nearly all of the glyphs have been significantly altered from the regular to the italic version.

Italic or Oblique?
Italic or Oblique?

Italic or Oblique?
Italic or Oblique?

Italic or Oblique?
Italic or Oblique?

Many perfectly respectable sans serif fonts have purely oblique versions for their italics, as these are relatively easy to create. Creating a true italic takes a lot of work, but if that's what you think your font needs, then you should definitely put in the effort.

Before you release an oblique font and call it an italic however, know that purists will gnash their teeth at the effrontery you've displayed. You can release an oblique family member labeled as an oblique if your heart tends toward the pure, but if you're releasing a sans serif family and you call your slanted fonts therein "italic," there's really nothing wrong with that—so says the impure heretic.

✳✳✳ *FontLab Tutorial*

HOW TO CREATE AN OBLIQUE FONT

Creating a purely oblique font is fairly easy in FontLab, as we will find out here.

1

Open up your finished regular font in FontLab. I can't stress "finished" enough—if you go through the effort of creating an oblique from a font you haven't finished, you may well have to go through the entire process again, after you've finished the regular font.

2

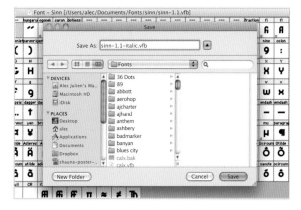

Save your regular font as a new font file. I have actually written over a perfectly good regular font file with an italic version, and the pain and suffering was appreciable.

3

Select all of your glyphs (cmd-A in the main window) and remove all hints from them. You'll have to re-hint all of the glyphs anyway after you slant them, so you might as well get rid of the hinting sooner rather than later. Save your work.

4

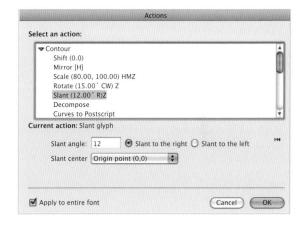

Go to the Tools menu, and choose Action to open up the Action window. Expand the choices under Contour and select Slant. (The default value of 12° is generally a good slant angle, but feel free to change the value here to your needs.) Check the Apply to Entire Font checkbox to apply your action to every glyph in your font.

Continues...

5

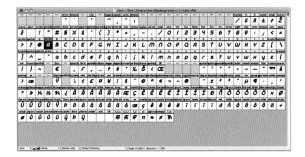

Click OK. FontLab asks if you're sure. Tell it you are.

6

Save your font again. You now have an oblique version of your glyphs. If you're making a true italic version, and not just an oblique, you have a lot more editing work yet to go. But that's beyond the scope of this book. Just be sure to study other fonts and their italics before you create your own.

7

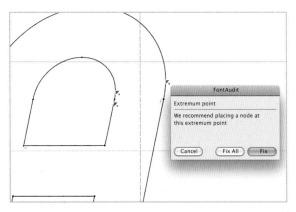

Make sure the Audit layer is turned on, and, get ready, go into every glyph of your font and check for problems. Slanting your glyphs changes things like extrema points—a point that was on the rightmost point of a glyph's arc might not be anymore after you've slanted the whole thing. And FontLab loves having extrema points on your glyphs. It can even turn straight lines into curves that you should straighten out again. Slanting your glyphs will likely create problems that you can inspect and fix by showing the Audit layer.

8

Autohint your font, as detailed in the previous section, Hinting.

9

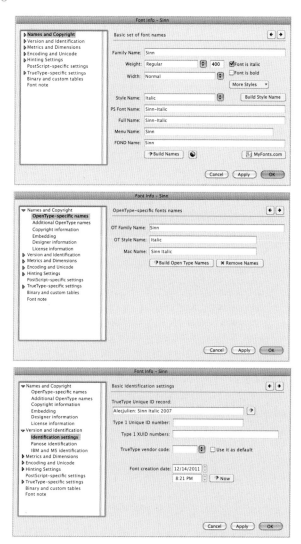

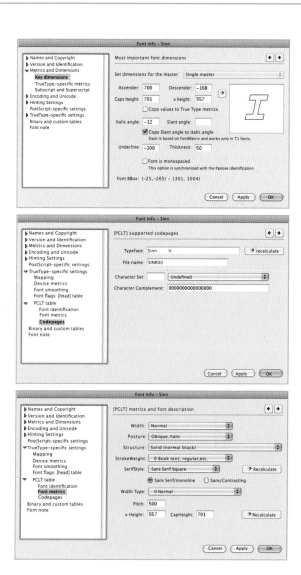

Open the Font Info window, and step through it just like you did for the regular font (as detailed in the previous section, Compiling Your Font). Shown here are some of the key screens that will be different from the info for your regular font. You can then generate your font!

✳✳✳ *FontLab Tutorial*

BOLD

Now let's tackle creating a bold font family member from a regular cousin.

1

Open up your regular font in FontLab, and save it as a new font file. Remove all hinting from the font, then save it again.

2

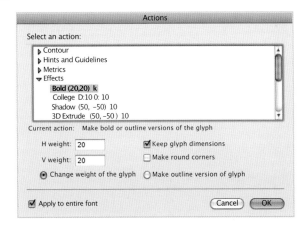

Go to the Tools menu, and choose Action to open up the Action window. Expand the choices under Effects and select Bold. (The default value of 20 for H Weight and V Weight is generally a good choice, but feel free to change the value here to your needs.)

3

space	exclam	quotedbl	numbersign	dollar	percent	ampersand	quotesingle
	!	"	#	$	%	&	'
parenleft	**parenright**	**asterisk**	**plus**	**comma**	**hyphen**	**period**	**slash**
(	)	✳	+	,	–	.	/
zero	**one**	**two**	**three**	**four**	**five**	**six**	**seven**
O	I	2	3	4	5	6	7
eight	**nine**	**colon**	**semicolon**	**less**	**equal**	**greater**	**question**
8	9	:	;	<	=	>	?
at	**A**	**B**	**C**	**D**	**E**	**F**	**G**
@	A	B	C	D	E	F	G
H	**I**	**J**	**K**	**L**	**M**	**N**	**O**
H	I	J	K	L	M	N	O

Font – Sinn [/Users/alec/Documents/Fonts/sinn/sinn-1.1.vfb]

space	exclam	quotedbl	numbersign	dollar	percent	ampersand	quotesingle
	!	"	#	$	%	&	'
parenleft	**parenright**	**asterisk**	**plus**	**comma**	**hyphen**	**period**	**slash**
(	)	✳	+	,	–	.	/
zero	**one**	**two**	**three**	**four**	**five**	**six**	**seven**
O	I	2	3	4	5	6	7
eight	**nine**	**colon**	**semicolon**	**less**	**equal**	**greater**	**question**
8	9	:	;	<	=	>	?
at	**A**	**B**	**C**	**D**	**E**	**F**	**G**
@	A	B	C	D	E	F	G
H	**I**	**J**	**K**	**L**	**M**	**N**	**O**
H	I	J	K	L	M	N	O

Font – Sinn [/Users/alec/Desktop/family/sinn-1.1-bold.vfb]

Check the "Apply to entire font" checkbox to apply your action to every glyph in your font.

4

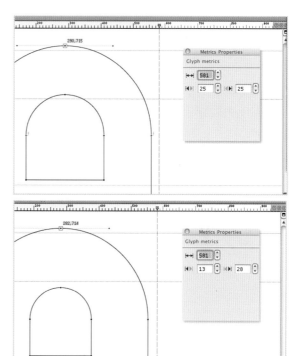

Before you get too excited, creating a bold font isn't generally as easy as creating an oblique. So it's not quite time to start hinting, setting properties, and compiling.

FontLab's bold action can do some strange things to your glyphs. For one thing, it tends to vertically shrink your glyphs. In the example I've been using (my font Sinn), going from regular to bold via FontLab's bold action has moved the top node of my "A" from 715 to 714—a minimal change, but one you'll probably want to fix. Also, note that the sidebearings are significantly different after FontLab's action—they've gone from 25 on both sides to 13 on the left and 28 on the right. You'll definitely want to fix that.

Continues…

5

ABCDEFG
ABCDEFG
ABCDEFG
ABCDEFG

One point to consider along these lines is how you want your bold font to be spaced in general. Most bold fonts, intuitively, take up more horizontal space than their regular counterparts. There are those that don't as well. Your job, as a font designer, is to think about how your bold font should be spaced relative to your regular version. Should it have the exact same sidebearings? This would make it wider than the regular font in page layout, but would keep the same amount of whitespace in between glyphs. Should it have wider sidebearings? This would make the bold version wider still in page layout, and increase the whitespace in between glyphs. Narrower sidebearings? This would make the bold version approach the same width as the regular, but would make the glyphs look tighter together in page layout. The image here shows News Gothic Std, regular and bold (top); and Marydale, regular and bold (bottom). News Gothic bold is wider in page layout than its regular counterpart. Marydale bold is almost exactly the same width as Marydale regular in page layout, which means its sidebearings are narrower.

6

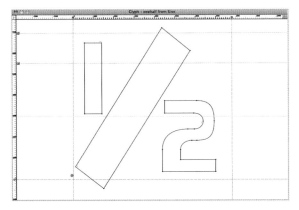

Another oddity of FontLab's bold action is that occasionally it will miss some parts of glyphs. For instance, in this screenshot the "½" glyph has had its slash properly bolded, but not the numeral parts of it. You'll have to bold these manually.

7

BOLD

BOLD

BOLD

BOLD

8

BOLD

BOLD

BOLD

BOLD

FontLab's bold action is really just a starting point for you to generate a bold font. It takes all parts of your glyphs and expands them uniformly. However, for many font families, bold family members are not expanded uniformly, but are rather expanded more horizontally than vertically. Most bold versions of fonts have thicker vertical stems than they do horizontal. In this image, the top example is Akzidenz Grotesk, the second is Akzidenz Grotesk artificially bolded uniformly, much as FontLab's bold action would do, and the third is Akzidenz Grotesk's real bold version. The real bold and artificial bold are overlaid to show the differences between them. Notice that the artificial bold is less appealing for a number of reasons, including all-around clumsiness, for lack of a better term. One telltale sign of a problem is that the whitespace in the artificial "B" is way too small compared with the whitespace of the "O" and "D."

There are notable exceptions to this—many handwriting fonts have bold versions that are uniformly bolder than their regular counterparts, for instance. The image here shows Marydale, an artificially bolded Marydale, and the real Marydale Bold. The two bold fonts are overlaid one on top of the other to show the slight differences between them. If you actually took Marydale and applied the FontLab bold action it would be almost indistinguishable from the real bold version. The artificial bolding I did here was in Adobe Illustrator.

Continues...

9

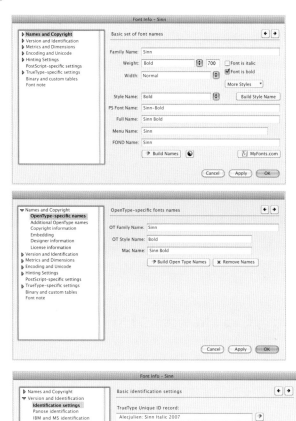

Once you have made all of your design decisions, and corrected the problems FontLab has created with your bold font, it's time to do as in the previous section, Compiling Your Font, and turn on the audit layer, fix those issues, autohint the font, and step through the Font Info screens before generating your bold face. Shown here are some of the key screens that will be different from the info for your regular font.

BOLD ITALIC

If you have a font that uses an oblique as its italic, the best way to create a bold italic family member is to take your bold font and italicize it, using the steps in this tutorial.

However, if you have a font that uses a true italic, your life is going to be significantly more difficult as you make your bold italic. If you bold your italic using FontLab's bold action, you're going to have to fix all of FontLab's problems; if you italicize your bold, you'll have all of the work of creating the italic flourishes and details all over again. One way or the other, you've got some work ahead of you.

Bigger families

Lots of font families are released with just bold, italic, and bold italic versions, and no others. If you'd like to make a bigger family, there are huge vistas in front of you. The first fonts you could tackle are condensed and expanded versions—fonts that are respectively narrower or wider than their regular cousins. You'll then want to develop a condensed bold font, a condensed italic, and a condensed bold italic, plus an extended bold, extended italic, and extended bold italic.

Keep in mind that, as with a bold font, making a condensed, extended, or expanded font is not just a matter of scaling its regular cousin. The top row of image 1 shows Akzidenz Grotesk Regular, followed by the same font simply expanded along the x-axis in Illustrator, and then Akzidenz Grotesk Extended on the bottom row. The middle version is unbalanced with the vertical strokes being too thick relative to the horizontal. In image 2, the top row is Akzidenz Grotesk Regular and the bottom is Akzidenz Grotesk Condensed. The middle row is Akzidenz Grotesk narrowed in Adobe Illustrator by simply condensing it along the x-axis. The vertical strokes in the middle version are proportionately too thick compared with the horizontal strokes. The actual condensed version of Akzidenz is perfectly balanced horizontally and vertically.

It's a huge selling point for a font to be released with lots of family members—but it's also a huge amount of work. There are even more possibilities open to you—more weights could include thin, medium, and black, and you could also have more widths.

A word of wisdom before you dive into making a super family including all of these weights and widths: make sure you are happy with your regular font before creating all of its cousins. The amount of work you'll be putting in to make varying versions will be huge enough without you changing the basis for the whole family and having to recreate all the cousins all over again.

1

EXPANDED
EXPANDED
EXPANDED

2

CONDENSED
CONDENSED
CONDENSED

Fontographer

As discussed earlier in the book, FontLab is not the only font creation tool out there. Although it falls short as a complete font creation tool, Fontographer is an excellent drawing tool that many designers swear by.

✳✳✱ *Fontographer Tutorial*
MAIN FEATURES OF FONTOGRAPHER

2

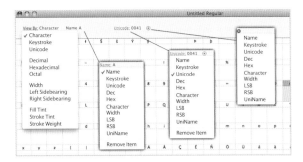

Near the top of the main screen, there are a series of useful drop-down menus. The left-most drop-down lets you change what gets displayed above each cell in the glyph matrix. Subsequent drop-downs display further information about whatever glyph you happen to have selected in the glyph matrix.

1

When you fire up Fontographer and create a new font, you're presented with a screen similar to FontLab's, with a matrix of blank glyph cells.

3

To edit/create a glyph, just double-click on the corresponding cell in Fontographer's main screen, and it opens up an editing window.

4

1.			11.	

1. selection tool
2. rectangle tool
3. oval tool
4. calligraphy pen tool
5. knife tool
6. corner point tool
7. rotate tool
8. scale tool
9. measurement tool
11. hand tool

12. multigon tool
13. line tool
14. pen toll
15. curve point tool
16. tangent point tool
17. flip tool
18. skew tool
19. magnification tool
20. convex arc tool

The tools available for drawing in Fontographer should be familiar to you if you've used FontLab. There are a couple of interesting tools the likes of which you might not have seen. For instance, the calligraphy pen tool lets you draw directly in a glyph editing window with a virtual calligraphy pen. If you have a pen tablet hooked up to your computer, you could use the calligraphy pen tool to interesting effect. The perspective tool, as another example, lets you rotate shapes in 3D around an imaginary axis.

5

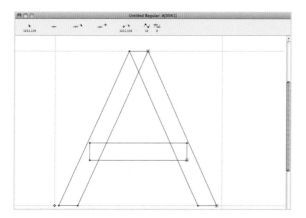

The rectangle tool works just as in FontLab. Here's an "A" drawn with rectangles. You can select multiple nodes just as in FontLab, by clicking and dragging your mouse over them, or by single-clicking on one at a time and holding the Shift key as you select more. Once nodes are selected, you can drag them with the mouse, or nudge them using the arrow keys on your keyboard.

6

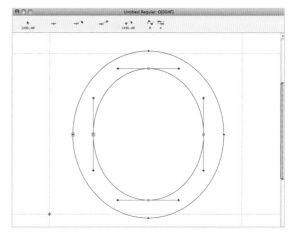

The oval tool works just as in FontLab. Here is an "O" drawn with two ovals.

7

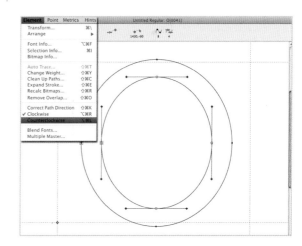

One difference here between Fontographer and FontLab—there is no command to remove overlaps in Fontographer. In order to hollow out the center of this "O" you select the inner oval and change its direction.

Continues…

8

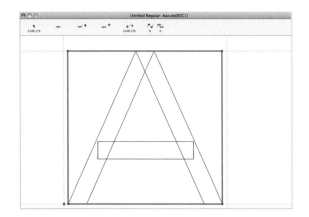

As with FontLab, Fontographer lets you create composite glyphs, wherein a new glyph can be composed of two already existing glyphs. Any changes you make to the original glyphs will be reflected in the composites. For example, say you already have an "A" and an acute. If you highlight the "A" in the main screen, you can choose Copy Component from the Edit menu, and your "A" is copied as a component.

9

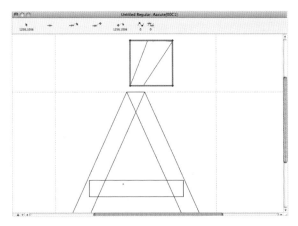

Now if you go to the A-acute cell of the main screen and double click on it to open up the edit window, you can paste your "A" component. Note the border around the component—that means that it's a live copy of your "A," and any changes you make to your "A" will be reflected here in this glyph.

10

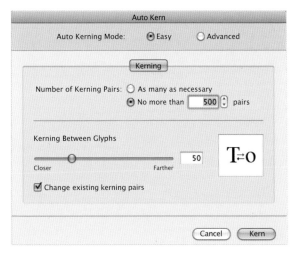

Go back to the main screen and select your acute to copy it as a component, then go back to your A-acute glyph and paste this into it. You now have two separate components in your A-acute. Changes you make to either of the original "A" or acute glyphs will be immediately reflected in your A-acute.

11

Auto Kern

Auto Kerning Mode: ● Easy   ○ Advanced

Kerning

Number of Kerning Pairs: ○ As many as necessary
● No more than 500 pairs

Kerning Between Glyphs

Closer —————————— Farther   50   T⇌o

☑ Change existing kerning pairs

Cancel   Kern

Fontographer provides a couple of options for kerning your font. Select "Auto Kern" to have Fontographer do the bulk of the work.

12

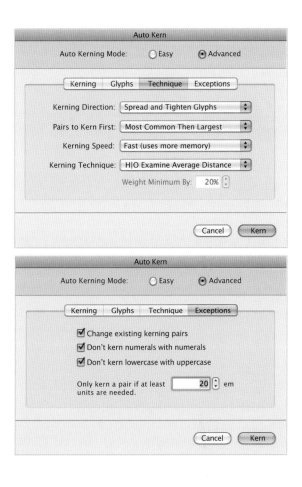

In advanced mode you get four screens of settings to tweak, which gives you a great deal of latitude in how Fontographer handles kerning.

Continues...

13

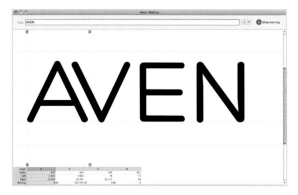

As with any automated process, Fontographer's auto kerning doesn't do a perfect job. You'll have to tweak its results by hand.

14

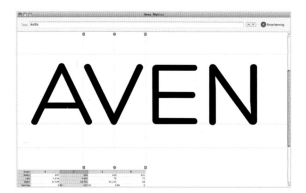

Go to the Window menu, and select Open Metrics Window. A kerning window much like the one in FontLab's appears. Unlike FontLab's version, if you just click on and drag the glyph you want to kern, it actually changes the glyph's sidebearings instead of its kerning. To actually change the kerning, you have to click on the "K" in a circle above the glyph and drag that to the left or right.

15

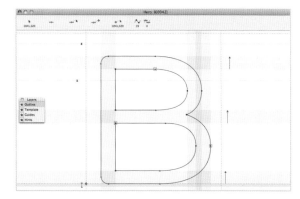

Fontographer also provides an autohinting mechanism. To invoke it, simply go to the Hints menu and select Autohint. This autohinting is on a glyph-by-glyph basis—that is, you can turn it on or off for one glyph at a time, for whichever glyph you have selected in the main screen. To see the hinting in action, make sure the Hints layer is clicked in the layers palette.

16

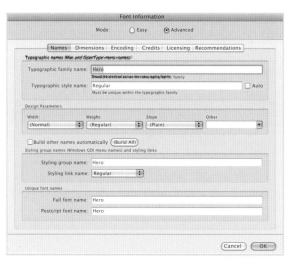

When it comes time to generate an actual font file from Fontographer, the process is similar to that of FontLab's. One thing you should do before you actually generate a font file is to make sure all of your font's information is correctly detailed in the proper place; and that place is the Font Info screen. To get there, go to the Element menu and select Font Info.

17

To generate a font file once all of your information is properly entered, simply go to the File menu and select Generate Font Files. You'll be presented with a basic dialog box that lets you generate font files.

DISADVANTAGES OF FONTOGRAPHER

So, we've got a great drawing tool complete with a full-featured editor and composite glyphs, good kerning and hinting tools, and a way to generate useable font files. What's the downside? Well, for one thing, although the kerning tools do let you set up implicit classes for kerning purposes (grouping like glyphs together so that they all get kerned the same way), there's no explicit mechanism in Fontographer for setting up OpenType classes the way you can in FontLab. The bigger issue, though, is that there is no way to include all of the nifty OpenType features that we've been through in our dealings with FontLab—ligatures, alternates, figures, swashes, etc. You'll have to leave these out of your Fontographer-developed fonts.

Of course, you could design your fonts in Fontographer, and then export them into FontLab (or other programs) to include OpenType features. There are designers who work this way. It just depends on your threshold for a forked workflow.

Aaron Bell

Passionate about Asian languages and cultures, Aaron Bell earned a B.A. in Asian Studies with a minor in Japanese.

He later graduated from the University of Reading with an M.A. in Typeface Design, developing a typeface aimed at Korean-Latin multi-script typesetting. Currently, he is employed on the Windows Font Team at Microsoft, focusing on East Asian scripts.

Do you remember your first font?

"The first font I developed was in a typography class using an online application called Fontstruct. Using a grid system and predefined square designs, it was easy to feel in control and gave me the confidence to explore. With that newfound drive, I decided to see how far I could push the design and made a typeface some 30 units high (most were 10 to 15).

I began my first 'real' type design at the University of Reading, in the Masters of Typeface Design program. Though I felt ready to design an awesome typeface, I couldn't have imagined my experiences of the next eight months and how much I would change and grow as a designer. Of course, once one begins a non-Latin script, everything changes again and you have to relearn from the very beginning. It isn't for the faint of heart."

How did you decide to design Korean fonts?

"I was an Asian Studies major in college, so it is an area in which I've long had an interest. I wanted to try something new and thought, naively, that the component-driven nature of Korean would allow me to produce a full character set within eight months. I learned, very quickly, how wrong I was!"

What are the challenges particular to designing Korean fonts—or more generally, CJK (Chinese, Japanese, and Korean) fonts?

"The greatest challenge is gaining the eye to see proportion and balance. Korean, Chinese, and Japanese are scripts comfortable in both vertical and horizontal alignment so their balance and proportion can be hard to grasp for a non-native designer. Furthermore, each script in CJK is different—it is difficult for Chinese people to design Korean and vice versa. Similarly, in many cases, the same glyph in a typeface for a Chinese audience and one for a Japanese audience will be designed differently since regional preferences for balance and proportion aren't the same.

The second is to understand the relationship between the CJK script and Latin. They must be designed to work together. If you design one script without considering the other, sacrifices must be made for them to work together. The only proper solution is to design both at the same time. However, since the price of a CJK font is prohibitive for 99% of all projects, it is much easier to simply license a CJK font that matches 'close enough.'

The third core issue is accessibility. Knowledge about designing CJK fonts is almost entirely in the native script. If you don't speak the language, it is hard to understand books written on the subject and study the process. I was lucky enough to gain access to several heavily illustrated books that allowed me to study the proportion and balance of Korean."

What general lessons about font creation could you share with a beginner?

"Don't forget the analogue. It is so easy to just start working on the computer or only draw the typeface once before working in a font design tool. However, at the beginning, it is especially hard to control the points and curves. So you'll make change after change without seeing much improvement. What I ended up doing was to sketch, scan, digitize, print out, and repeat."

Do you have an idea before you start drawing glyphs, or do you sit down and see what happens?

"It really depends. Usually when I draw glyphs, I have a sense of certain qualities I want the drawing to have—say, high contrast, and squarish features. These qualities can be of my own devising, or can be inspired by a bit of lettering or type that I've seen and want to explore, but they're always based in something. That said, doodling letters is a whole lot of fun and it is interesting to just experiment and see what happens."

"In terms of sales models, there is always room for experimentation."

In terms of sales models, there is always room for experimentation. Jos Buivenga gave away a single weight of Museo for free, encouraging folk to purchase other weights when that first was not sufficient, and he's done quite well with it. Others charge high prices to establish exclusivity or throw in with large storehouse websites for the sake of simplicity. I think this sort of variation will always exist since there is no single, right method of selling type.

The market can definitely support the number of new fonts. But the number of positions as full-time type designers are few and many find themselves doing it as a side business to something else. Again, it isn't to say designers shouldn't aspire to type-design careers, but to understand it might be hard to get into immediately. We change fashion every year and that's never caused problems, so fonts are the same."

"Of course, once one begins a non-Latin script, everything changes again and you have to relearn from the very beginning. It isn't for the faint at heart."

How do you start the font creation process?

"I start with pencil and paper. It is the fastest way to get a sense of what a letterform might look like. Of course, the digitization step will change things significantly, so it is important to return to drawing again and again to make sure the design is going in the right direction. Otherwise it is too easy to become entrenched in the digital version, which may or may not be the ideal design solution."

Do you have any thoughts about the future of the font business?

"One of the most defining changes of our age is the shift from centralized type designers to long-distance ones—the old model of everyone working in the same building is no longer necessary. I'm not sure if large publishers will continue to dominate the field or if smaller publishers and type foundries can establish names for themselves.

Aaron Bell

1.

> "**Stay awhile,**
> *Reverend sir,*
> LET ME
> **ask you**
> where you go."

From a poem by
Chong Ch'ol
(1536–1593)

Translation by
The Sejong Society

저
중아
개 있거라
니 가는데
물어보자

2.

Named after the Korean word for Lion, Saja is an upright, contemporary serif typeface designed especially for long-form, multi-script typesetting of Latin and Korean. Aimed at magazine usage, Saja walks the line between quiet and quirky, bringing a refreshing air to the page.

Saja includes a regular and book text as well as paired bolds for each. As Korean tends to be set at a lighter weight than Latin, this innovative design allows comfortable text setting for both scripts. Furthermore, Saja introduces a new paradigm to the field of Korean typography—the true italic. No more will Korean typographers be forced to mechanically slant text for emphasis, but can use a brand new style that is still just as easy to read.

3.

Saja

1. Saja: an upright, serif face designed for dual-script typesetting (Latin and Korean), this font introduces true italic to Korean typography.

2. Saja: includes a regular and book text, as well as paired bolds for each. Korean tends to be set lighter than Latin and this allows comfortable text setting for both scripts.

3. Saja: named with the Korean word for lion.

Going Pro

CHAPTER 5
MARKETING AND
SELLING YOUR
FONTS

COPYRIGHTING
YOUR FONTS
P.172

COMMERCIAL
SELLING AND
LICENSING
P.174

WEB
FONTS
P.186

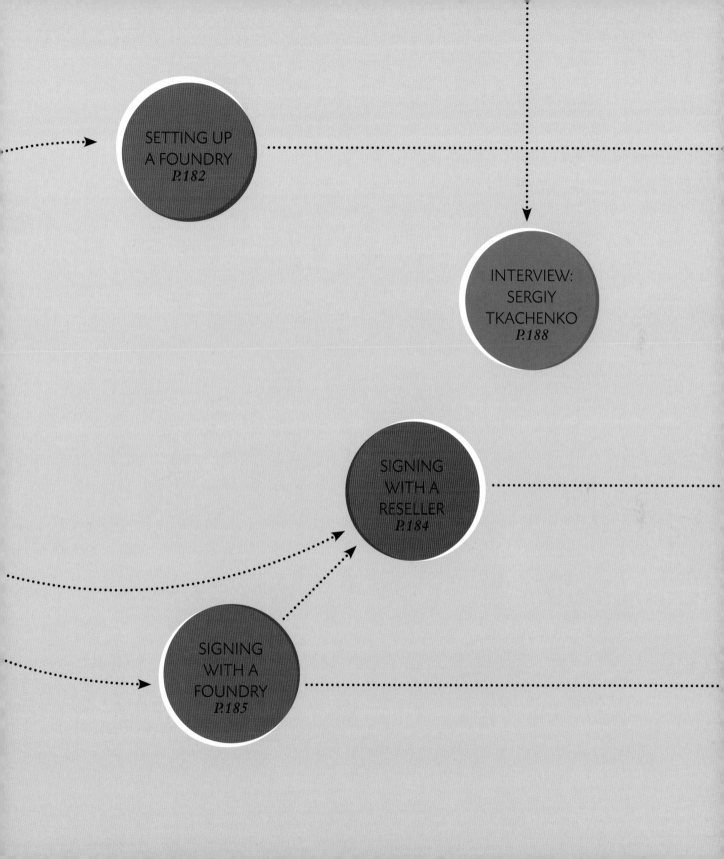

Copyrighting your fonts

How do you legally protect your fonts from being copied and released by someone else as their own work? First of all, I have to make the standard disclaimer: I am not a lawyer. I am also more familiar with the legal situation in the United States than the rest of the world. So take what I say with a grain of salt and make sure to consult a legal authority if you're genuinely concerned about protecting your fonts.

That said, here's the basic gist in the United States. The shapes of your glyphs are not copyrightable. Bitmap versions of your fonts are not copyrightable. However, your fonts as scalable font files are indeed copyrightable.

The U.S. Copyright Office allows one to copyright "pictorial, graphic, or sculptural work," but in a 1979 decision it was ruled that a typeface (the actual shapes of your font's glyphs) does not fall under these categories. In other words, the shapes of glyphs don't count as art—in the eyes of the law, they are just something used by artists to create copyrightable art. And the mere act of digitizing glyphs does not, in the eyes of the Copyright Office, make a typeface copyrightable.

However, a scalable font file is another thing entirely. One thing about fonts is that they are always editable in a font-editing program such as FontLab. I can buy any font I like, and open it in FontLab. And once I have it open in FontLab, there's nothing stopping me from altering it, changing the name of it and the authorship/copyright information in the font, and generating a "new" font.

There was a landmark case in 1998 over just this issue, when Adobe successfully sued a font developer who had taken some of Adobe's fonts and opened them in a font-editing program, altered them (minimally), and released them as his own creations. The eventual ruling was that a font file can be thought of as a small computer program, complete with code that generates scalable shapes, and computer programs are indeed copyrightable. So while the shapes of your glyphs are not themselves copyrightable, the code in your font file that generates those shapes is indeed protectable.

Generally speaking, in the U.S., computer programs are copyrightable as works of text. That's presumably because you can generally print out the code of your computer program and send it as a text file to the Copyright Office. Of course, the code behind your fonts is not readily printable— there's no step-by-step list of instructions for your font that FontLab allows you to print out. So, to be honest, I'm not sure what exactly you'd send in to the Copyright Office if you were to submit your font for protection.

Which tells you that I haven't filed any of my fonts with the Copyright Office. Why not, you might ask? Well, for one thing, simply by generating your font you get some minimal amount of copyright protection in the U.S. (It really is fairly minimal, and if you're concerned you should really file for actual protection.) But the bigger factor for me is that my fonts are sold worldwide—as yours will be. I don't have the resources to try to legally protect my fonts across hundreds of countries.

ILLEGAL USAGE

At any rate, by far the greater concern for most font creators is piracy. I've never run across one of my fonts that has been reworked or relabeled and sold as a different product. (I have seen a couple of instances of this from other designers over the last few years, but it seems to be a fairly rare phenomenon.) However, I have run across plenty of examples of my fonts being bundled and offered illegally for download on torrent sites. Unfortunately, there's really not much that can be done legally about these sorts of pirates. It doesn't matter what sorts of copyright protections you possess, pirates will remain active, anonymous, and virtually untouchable.

USEFUL WEBSITES

Copyright law varies from country to country, so it's worth checking out the rules that could affect your fonts.

Australia Copyright Council
www.copyright.org.au

Canadian Intellectual Property Office
www.cipo.ic.gc.ca

Directory of Intellectual Property Offices
www.wipo.int/directory/en/urls.jsp

European Union Copyright Office
www.eucopyright.com

UK Copyright Office
www.ipo.gov.uk

US Library of Congress Office
www.copyright.gov

PATENTS

If you're genuinely concerned about protecting your fonts legally from those who would try to rework or relabel your creations, you should look into patents. As this webpage from Harvard University notes: "Patenting is becoming the method of choice for effective protection of original computer programs. Whereas a copyright protects an original work in the tangible fixed form in which it has been set down, a patent protects the creation of inventive concepts as well as their reduction to practice." (www.techtransfer.harvard.edu/inventions/ip/software/compare)

The U.S. patent process is more complicated and expensive than the copyright process, and if you want to go down this route, you should definitely talk with a lawyer who specializes in this area. Also you should consider the economics involved—if you are going to spend $1000 patenting your font (a figure I'm picking out of thin air, by the way), you might want to consider if you think you're going to make back that money in sales of your font. If your font will sell for $10, that's 100 copies, if you're getting 100% of the sales from your font (which you won't get). Don't take for granted that you'll sell that many copies; and even if you do, remember that that is just your breakeven point. Of course, in the unlikely event that a font of yours is illegally reworked, and you own a patent on it, you might do well financially if you bring a suit against the transgressor, and the transgressor is rich. But that is an extremely improbable scenario.

Commercial selling and licensing

Generally speaking, fonts are not sold, they're licensed. Much like a great deal of the movies and music you "buy," in actuality the sellers of these media are really granting you a license to use the media for specific purposes; and, on the flip side of this, these licenses generally forbid you from doing other things with the media in question. With fonts, it boils down to a few key issues for you as the seller of the font.

1. To what sort of uses can the font be put?

Can the font be used in commercial projects? I certainly hope you'll allow this for your fonts, but there are some font creators who either don't allow this, or allow it under a separate, usually more expensive, license. All kinds of commercial projects? Print? Web? Items for sale? Interactive items?

2. How many users are allowed to use the font under the license?

Often a font will be licensed on a per-user basis—that is, one license will often be good for one user. The idea is that an organization should buy more than one license if there will be more than one person using the font at any one time. Some font licenses are more liberal and will be good for, say, up to five users per license—that is, an organization could buy one license and have five of its members use your font at any one time, under the terms of the license.

3. How many copies can be made of the font under the license?

Sometimes licenses will address the issue of making copies of your font. Generally, you want your font's users to be able to make backup copies of your font, but not be able to make huge numbers of copies and store them wherever they like. The more copies someone makes, the more likely it is that copies will find their way to unlicensed users. Of course, this is one of those things that is almost completely unenforceable, so you might not want to spend a lot of time worrying about it.

4. Can the font be embedded in PDFs and other documents?

PDFs and some other sorts of documents can embed copies of your fonts within them, so that printing bureaus don't need separate copies of your fonts in order to actually print these documents. It's up to you whether or not to allow this sort of activity via your font's license. I recommend being very lenient along these lines, since this practice truly helps designers and printers use your fonts. You want to be accommodating to your font's users, so they'll keep coming back for more of your fonts in the future.

5. Can a copy of the font be given to printing agencies for use with the licensee's documents?

Regardless of embeddability, some printing bureaus want a copy of the actual font, not just an embedded version of it, in order to print design files. It's once again up to you to decide whether or not to allow this practice. In theory, the printer uses the font throughout the project being printed, and once the project is done, deletes the font from their computers forever. The project gets done correctly, and there are no rogue copies of your font floating around, being used by unlicensed individuals. You could specify this exactly in your font's license, if that's what you want to happen. Of course, this is another area where whatever you put in your license, people will abuse it from time to time. Some printing bureaus and other agencies will keep your font on their computers and use it at their whim, without paying any licensing fees to you.

6. Can the font be embedded in web pages?

We are at the dawn of the era of decent web typography, and now through services such as TypeKit, FontDeck, MyFonts.com, Fonts.com, Google, and others, you can license fonts to use on websites. Which means that you, a font creator, have the chance to potentially profit from this relatively new use of your fonts. In crafting your license, you want to account for this possibility. Does a person licensing your font automatically get the right to embed that font on their web pages? Or is this a separate license for which they should be paying extra? As an example of this distinction, MyFonts.com licenses many of their fonts for web use, but this is generally under a separate license from the standard use license—in fact, as a purchaser, you have to add fonts to your shopping cart in separate steps in order to purchase a standard license and then a web license.

7. Can the font be embedded in software?

Programmers can, in some software development environments, embed fonts in their programs, to be used in the programs by end users. Since these end users will likely not be licensed users of your font, you have to account for this possibility in your license. Will it be allowed? Allowed for an extra price? Not allowed at all?

8. Can the font be altered by the licensee?

This is a rarer item to put into a license, but is at the least something you should ponder. What if I buy one of your fonts and decide that the em dash is too wide for my tastes? So I fire up FontLab, open your font, shrink the em dash, recompile the font, and reinstall it on my system. Is this OK in your eyes, or are you so wedded to the shape of your font's glyphs that the idea of someone else tweaking them is entirely distasteful to you? You can specify this in your license. You should also specify in this section of your license things that may seem obvious, for example, that people should not take your font, tweak it, and resell it as a new face.

MYFONTS LICENSE

Here's a standard (non-web font) license used for a font for sale at MyFonts.com.

1. Allowed uses

You may use the licensed fonts to create images on any surface such as computer screens, paper, web pages, photographs, movie credits, printed material, T-shirts, and other surfaces where the image is a fixed size. You may use the licensed fonts to create EPS files or other scalable drawings provided that such files are only used by the household or company licensing the font.

2. Number of users

The maximum number of simultaneous users is specified in the applicable receipt. All users must belong to the same company or household purchasing the font.

3. Third parties

You may provide the font to a graphic designer, printer or other service bureau that is working on your behalf only if they agree to use the font exclusively for your work, agree to the terms of this license, and retain no copies of the font on completion of the work. You may not provide the font or make it accessible to any other third parties.

4. Embedding

You may embed the licensed fonts into any document you send to third parties. Such documents may be viewed and printed (but not edited) by the recipients. You may not under any circumstances embed the licensed fonts into software or hardware products in which the fonts will be used by the purchasers of such products. Such use requires a different license which may be offered by the Foundry through MyFonts. Please contact help@myfonts.com for further information.

5. Modifications

You may import characters from the font as graphical objects into a drawing program and modify such graphical objects. You may not modify, adapt, translate, reverse engineer, decompile, disassemble, or create derivative works based on the licensed font itself without Foundry's prior written consent.

Continues…

6. Copyright

The font and the accompanying materials are copyrighted and contain proprietary information and trade secrets belonging to the foundry owning the font. Unauthorized copying of the Product even if modified, merged, or included with other software, or of the written materials, is expressly forbidden. You may be held legally responsible for any infringement of the foundry's intellectual property rights that is caused or encouraged by your failure to abide by the terms of this Agreement.

7. Termination

This Agreement is effective until terminated. This Agreement will terminate automatically without notice from MyFonts or the Foundry if you fail to comply with any provision contained herein. Upon termination, you must destroy the written materials, the Product, and all copies of them, in part and in whole, including modified copies, if any.

8. Product Upgrades

MyFonts may, from time to time, update the Product. Product upgrade pricing may apply.

9. Disclaimer and Limited Warranty

MyFonts warrants the Product to be free from defects in materials and workmanship under normal use for a period of twenty one (21) days from the date of delivery as shown on your receipt.

MyFonts' entire liability and your exclusive remedy as to a defective product shall be, at MyFonts' option, either return of purchase price or replacement of any such product that is returned to MyFonts with a copy of the invoice. MyFonts shall have no responsibility to replace the product or refund the purchase price if failure results from accident, abuse, or misapplication, or if any product is lost or damaged due to theft, fire, or negligence. Any replacement product will be warranted for twenty-one (21) days. This warranty gives you specific legal rights. You may have other rights, which vary from state to state.

EXCEPT AS EXPRESSLY PROVIDED ABOVE, THE PRODUCT, IS PROVIDED "AS IS," NEITHER MYFONTS NOR THE FOUNDRY MAKES ANY WARRANTY OF ANY KIND, EITHER EXPRESSED OR IMPLIED, INCLUDING, BUT NOT LIMITED TO THE IMPLIED WARRANTIES OF MERCHANTABILITY AND FITNESS FOR A PARTICULAR PURPOSE.

The entire risk as to the quality and performance of the Product rests upon you. Neither MyFonts nor the Foundry warrants that the functions contained in the Product will meet your requirements or that the operation of the software will be uninterrupted or error free.

NEITHER MYFONTS NOR THE FOUNDRY SHALL BE LIABLE FOR ANY DIRECT, INDIRECT, CONSEQUENTIAL, OR INCIDENTAL DAMAGES (INCLUDING DAMAGES FROM LOSS OF BUSINESS PROFITS, BUSINESS INTERRUPTION, LOSS OF BUSINESS INFORMATION, AND THE LIKE) ARISING OUT OF THE USE OF OR INABILITY TO USE THE PRODUCT EVEN IF MYFONTS OR THE FOUNDRY HAS BEEN ADVISED OF THE POSSIBILITY OF SUCH DAMAGES.

Because some states do not allow the exclusion or limitation of liability for consequential or incidental damages, the above limitation may not apply to you.

10. Governing Law

This agreement is governed by the laws of the United States of America and the Commonwealth of Massachusetts.

FREE FONTS

Licenses don't just apply to commercial fonts; free fonts should have licenses too. Even if you're releasing one of your fonts free of charge, it should still have a license attached to it that details what users can and can't do with the font.

Why would you release a font for free? Many reasons. Perhaps you're just the benevolent type and enjoy seeing your work used, regardless of the financial compensation you receive from it. Or perhaps your beneficence is mixed with pragmatism, and you realize that if you give away, say, one member of an entire font family, people might download it, use it, and fall in love with it, then come back and buy the rest of your family to use with it. This is a tried and true strategy that many font creators use.

Jos Buivenga often releases one or two members of his font families as free fonts, and hopes that their users will see the value in coming back to buy the rest of the family members. Museo Slab, at the time of this writing, is available in one weight—the 500 weight—free of charge (image 1). The other family members are available for a very reasonable price should you choose to buy them.

OPEN-SOURCE FONTS

One other free license you might want to ponder: do you want to release your font as an open-source font? Not only are open-source fonts free to access, but also users can freely take your font and modify it to their heart's content, usually with the caveat that whatever they release stemming from your open-source font must also be released as an open-source font. The idea of open-source releases is usually that they're supposed to be viral in a sense— any branch of an open-source project should itself be open source in exactly the same way as its progenitor.

One such license that has already been developed and (hopefully) perfected is the SIL Open Font License, more information about which can be found here: http://scripts.sil.org/OFL. I've released two font families under the OFL and am happy I did so—I feel like what I've released has the potential to have an interesting and useful life of its own, well beyond whatever I choose to do with it.

Museo Slab 100
Museo Slab 100 Italic
Museo Slab 300
Museo Slab 300 Italic
Museo Slab 500
Museo Slab 500 Italic
Museo Slab 700
Museo Slab 700 Italic
Museo Slab 900
Museo Slab 900 Italic
Museo Slab 1000
Museo Slab 1000 Italic

Continues...

PRICING

How do you price your fonts, should you choose not to release them for free? In my personal experience, it has been something of an exercise in classic capitalism. Many of the fonts I released were set at a price that was too high, and I adjusted it downward until I hit the sweet spot where enough people were willing to pay the price to make it good value for both consumer and producer.

But where do you even begin? Research. Check out MyFonts.com to see what similar fonts to your own are going for. If some are more expensive than you'd think they should be, try to figure out why that is. Are they released with substantially more OpenType features (discretionary ligatures, etc) than their competition? Do they have substantially more family members, glyphs, or languages? Are they better constructed than others? Are they more popular than others? Try to figure out where your font family fits into this scheme. Are your fonts comparable to others like it or are there shortcomings? If there are shortcomings, then you might either have to price your fonts lower than the competition, or fix those shortcomings before you release your font. Even if there are no shortcomings, and your fonts have relatively the same number of features and glyphs as your competitors, you still might have to release your fonts at a lower price, if you are new to the field. Reputation and longevity have something to do with what people are willing to pay for fonts.

It's also a good idea to release a font or font family at a discounted price for the first few weeks of its existence. People love a bargain, and can be encouraged to buy a product they're on the fence about if they think they're getting a one-time deal that they may never see again. Fonts at MyFonts.com are often released with an initial discount between 10 and 50%. (Of course, if you're releasing your font at a relatively low price, a steep discount may mean you're making practically nothing on each license sold. Factor this into your considerations when pricing and setting an initial discount.)

There is a really surprising disparity in prices between fonts, so be prepared to puzzle through your pricing scheme for a while before coming up with the right price points. Some large families, clearly targeting design agencies and not individual users, are priced in the thousands of dollars for the entire family. Some families are priced much more modestly, to entice individual users—it's all about your target market. But if you're a new designer, don't expect that your font families are going to sell right away at a hefty price tag to large design agencies. My advice is to start relatively low and try to get some traction with individual designers. Once your fonts are generally respected in the design community, you can start developing expensive families, if that's the path you think is right for you.

One other thing to consider is marketed value versus perceived value. If you price your font at $10,000, you're trying to market the idea that there's something very special about your font—something that a similar $10 font can't offer. Of course, justifying that special something about your font will be a tall order, but if you can, and you can sell a few copies of it, you've done pretty well for yourself. On the other hand, say you take that same font and price it at $10. With that price tag you might be saying to consumers something along the lines of "this is an inexpensive font that you don't need to worry too much about buying. Even if it's not great, you're just out ten bucks. There's probably nothing special about it, but it might come in handy." Maybe you're hoping that you can sell a thousand copies of it with this marketing tactic.

Now of course the marketing value is only half of the story—there's the actual perceived value from the consumer's perspective. If you market your font as a unique $10,000 font, and buyers check into what you're offering and see that it has only 100 glyphs that aren't particularly well-crafted, and no OpenType features, then the perceived value of your font is not going to match the marketing value. And it will be a miracle if you sell any copies.

Pricing: an example from MyFonts.com

Let's take a little tour of MyFonts.com, looking for a font or font family for a wedding invitation. The first thing you'll notice after browsing through many script fonts suitable for wedding invitations is that their purchasing options can be somewhat confusing. Take, for example, the Tupelo font family. If you go to the buying choices page, the sheer number of choices is a bit intimidating.

But the font's creator has done an excellent job of explaining things on the font's main page: "Tupelo comes in two main fonts, plus a set of beginning lowercase, a set of ending lowercase, and plenty of alternates and extras. The non-pro set consists of five fonts, while Tupelo Pro combines the lot in a single font of over 840 characters, which includes programming for push-button swash caps, stylistic alternates, oldstyle figures, beginning and ending letters."

This tells potential buyers exactly what they need to know for when they get to the intimidating buying choices page. You can, if you want the entire set of available glyphs and features, either buy the pro version for $39.95, or buy all five of the non-pro family members, for a substantially higher price tag. Why would anyone buy the more expensive, non-pro version? Well, if you're a designer working with old or non-powerful software that doesn't support OpenType features (or you're a designer who doesn't realize what OpenType features are and how to use them), the pro version won't do you any good—all of those wonderful ligatures and alternate glyphs will be locked away inside the font, unavailable to your software. For this reason, many font creators will release separate pro versions, and then bundles of non-pro versions of their fonts as well.

Speaking of OpenType features, we can note that Tupelo Pro supports ligatures, stylistic alternates, swashes, and oldstyle figures (see image 1 and image 2 on following page).

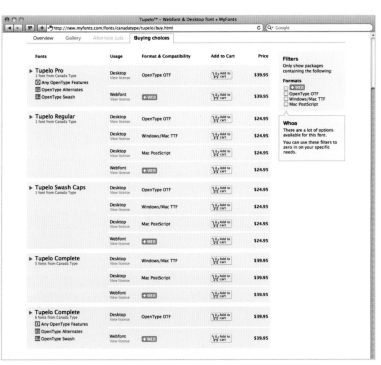

Continues…

Another font family suitable for wedding invitations is Aphrodite Pro, which for $37 buys you 481 glyphs, along with discretionary ligatures, ligatures, contextual alternates, stylistic alternates, historical forms, and swashes (image 3).

Penabico costs $79.90, but gives you a robust 2,048 glyphs, along with contextual alternates, discretionary ligatures, contextual ligatures, historical figures, initial forms, ligatures, medial forms, oldstyle figures, ornaments, small caps, swashes, and titling alternates (image 4). Also available in the family are sets of designed abbreviations (50 of them for $5.90), words (101 for $11.90), extras (42 of them for free), and ornaments (75 of them for $22.90).

Mousse Script Regular sells for $49, and comes with 307 glyphs, including discretionary ligatures, ligatures, and stylistic alternates (image 5). A set of alternate styles is $49 for another 209 glyphs. You can buy both together for $79.

Coming in at the low end of the price spectrum, we have Wild Song (image 6). It comes in three styles—thin, medium, and fat—for $19 each, or all three together for $45. Each font contains 283 glyphs, with OpenType features including capital spacing, discretionary ligatures, fractions, ligatures, and ordinals.

At the other end of the price spectrum, we have the lovely PF Champion Pro, which comes in two weights at $125 each, or both for $225 (image 7). Each font sports an absurd 4,299 glyphs and an array of OpenType features that puts other fonts to shame.

Origins features a single font for $39, and comes with 389 glyphs. OpenType features include ligatures and stylistic alternates (image 8).

Valliciergo has an impressive 999 glyphs and sells for $44 (image 9). OpenType features include contextual alternates, initial forms, ligatures, proportional figures, stylistic alternates, smallcaps, and swashes.

This should give you some idea of the range of prices and features that various fonts have. When you've spent hours and hours over weeks and months creating a font, and you're thinking that people should be paying you thousands of dollars for your painstaking work, remember to check and see what other fonts like yours can offer, and at what price.

5

8

6

9

7

Setting up your own foundry

It's all well and good to set prices for your fonts, but this won't be of much help to you if you can't figure out how to sell them.

So what are your options? There are, broadly, three ways to go about selling fonts. The first is to set up your own foundry and sell your own fonts on your own website. The second is to set up your own foundry and sell your fonts through a reseller. The third is to sign with someone else's foundry and let them handle font sales for you.

What does it mean to set up your own foundry? Well, in one sense, there's not much to it. Do a bit of research, find a foundry name that no one else is using, and do a little bit of branding. Voilà, you have a foundry.

Of course, if you want to get more serious about things, and have some protection under the law for your foundry, you'll want to talk to a lawyer and perhaps incorporate. In the United States, you can generally set up a Limited Liability Company (LLC) for a relatively small investment of time and money, and you will have limited personal liability for the debts and actions of the LLC, along with the possibility of tax benefits as well. There are also a variety of other corporate structures under which you could arrange your foundry. (In the U.S., the S-corporation and C-corporation are the usual suspects for incorporation; there are also many other corporate structures and business entity structures that can be used—sole proprietorships, partnerships, cooperatives, etc. Consult a lawyer and/or an accountant to see which might be right for you.)

NAMING YOUR FOUNDRY

Whatever business structure you decide upon, you should carefully vet available domain names and social media handles before you finalize a name for your foundry. A made-up word or an unexpected conjunction of terms is best for this, and means you'll run into the least possibility of naming conflicts with other foundries or other businesses in general.

Online services, such as namechk.com, make it simple to research available social media handles. I decided to see how available "Indolent Sandwich" is, and was surprised to find that several sites have already had "indolentsandwich" registered by someone (image 1). It's tough to come up with anything original!

My own foundry, Haiku Monkey, is a conjunction of terms quite unlikely to come up in anyone else's thoughts about naming a foundry. Running through some of the foundries that have popular fonts as I'm writing this, I see ActiveSphere, which is a nice random conjunction of terms. 4th February isn't a random conjunction of terms, but isn't exactly something that anyone else would come up with to refer to a foundry, and is thus a good choice for a foundry name. Other popular foundry names I see are slightly less safe from attempted duplication. Canada Type, NiceType, LatinoType, and Typocalypse are far more likely to run into attempted duplication of their names by new foundries. Of course, you could always just brand your foundry with your own name. Famous font designers Mark Simonson and Laura Worthington have done exactly this without relying on a catchy foundry name.

If you decide to name your foundry something both typographic and relatively general, for example, Best Fonts, and then go to buy the domain name bestfonts.com, you'll undoubtedly run into trouble, since that domain name is probably already taken. When I started Haiku Monkey, I was reasonably certain that haikumonkey.com, .net, and dot-anything-else were all available. And the same goes for social media handles. Try registering "bestfonts" at Twitter, and you'll probably be disappointed. So it's then up to you how attached you are to your name. Would it be worth it to you to live with a domain name like bestfontsfoundry.com? Or a Twitter handle of "bestfontsllc" or something similar?

SALES

Earlier, I mentioned that one way to sell your fonts is to start your own foundry and sell your fonts through your own website. This strategy has the advantage that you keep 100% of control and profits to yourself, but you should think long and hard about striking out on this path. One thing to consider carefully is dealing with e-commerce. It's one thing to set up a nice website to display your fonts; it's another thing entirely to deal with credit cards (and the inherent risk of fraud that comes with them), around-the-clock customer service (including refunds), SSL technologies and site certificates, shopping carts, and a million other e-commerce intricacies. That's not to mention the wrinkle that these costs will add to your operation and cut into that 100% of profit you thought you were keeping.

Also, there's the issue of marketing. If you let someone else sell your fonts for you, there's the implicit understanding that they can help significantly with the marketing of their site and your fonts on their site. If you go it alone, it's up to you to market your site and your fonts. Do you have a marketing background? Don't take such things for granted. Marketing is an arcane art, not to be taken lightly.

There's also the issue of credibility. If I don't know you and your work, I'm less likely to give up my credit card information on your website than I am on a site like MyFonts.com or Fonts.com.

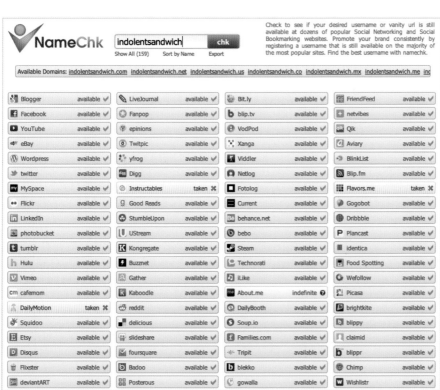

Signing with a reseller

Once you've set up a foundry, by far the easiest way to get started making money is to distribute your fonts through a font reseller. The biggest resellers out there at the moment are MyFonts. com and Fonts.com.

THE BENEFITS FOR YOU

Here's what these companies will do for you:

- Provide web pages on their sites detailing your fonts (providing images for customers to view, along with information about glyphs, OpenType features, etc.)

- Provide a 24-7 mechanism for e-commerce and customer service so that customers can buy your fonts any time of the day or night, and send questions to customer-service professionals about your fonts.

- Provide a spot on a site where thousands of people shop for fonts every day, meaning that your fonts have the chance of being seen by many eyes.

- Provide excellent search mechanisms (font names, styles, keywords/tags, etc.) so that your font can be found even if no one knows it exists.

- Provide mechanisms for setting up special offers, so that your font can attract extra attention by being put on sale or offered as part of some other special deal.

THE BENEFITS FOR RESELLERS

In return, resellers take a sizable percentage of the retail price. MyFonts.com and Fonts.com both, as of the time of writing, take 50% of the retail price. You could also take a couple of the above points that I think are positives and make them negatives, depending on your point of view. Perhaps you're not happy with the way the resellers configure their web pages, and you think you could create a much more beautiful way to display your wares. Perhaps you want customers talking to you about your fonts, not to some random customer-service rep who may not know anything about your work in particular. Perhaps the idea of your fonts being mixed in with thousands of others is not a positive, as you think your fonts will get lost in the mix.

If this is how you view the situation, and you're drawn to that magical 100% figure that you think you should be making, then by all means think about setting up your own retail site. But make sure you've thought it through carefully.

Also, you should know that there's nothing in most resellers' agreements with foundries that prohibits you from selling your fonts on their sites as well as on your own site, so you could do both if you're extraordinarily motivated. The general agreement for resellers is non-exclusive, though they do ask you not to price fonts lower than on their sites, which I think is pretty reasonable. Nobody is going to buy a font from MyFonts.com for $49 if they can buy it at indolentsandwich.com for $29.

The process for signing with a reseller is generally not too complicated. There's some paperwork to read and sign. As of right now, you can visit MyFonts.com at http://new.myfonts.com/info/prospectus, and Fonts.com: www.fonts.com/Contact/foundrysubmit.htm to get the latest information. Once the paperwork is done, it's simply a matter of uploading or emailing your fonts, along with some accompanying graphics, to the reseller. Boom—you're in business!

At the moment, MyFonts.com pays royalties monthly by electronic direct deposit. Fonts.com pays royalties quarterly via old-fashioned paper checks.

Signing with a foundry

If you release a font family to a foundry for release, it is generally an exclusive arrangement—you can't also release the font on your own website or through a reseller such as MyFonts.com. Check the contract to see if there's a timeframe on it to your liking—unless you want the exclusive arrangement to last for ever. Some foundries will help you complete your fonts, which brings an entirely new aspect into play. If you are not the exclusive designer, then perhaps a lifetime exclusivity clause makes sense. At any rate, these are issues you'll need to come to terms with.

As with a reseller, a foundry will grant you some percentage of royalties for each of your font licenses sold and will keep the rest. Unfortunately for you, this percentage might be the wholesale price, since the foundry might sell your font to a reseller—i.e., the profit is diluted more in this model than it would be if you were dealing directly with a reseller. Some foundries, on the contrary, will give their designers a percentage of the retail price; and some foundries deal exclusively through their own websites and not through resellers. Make sure you check into all of this in your negotiations.

ADVANTAGES AND DISADVANTAGES

What would you get out of signing with another foundry? Well, even more so than dealing with a reseller yourself, a foundry could take care of all of the business and marketing side of things for you. Also, some foundries are well known in the design community, and being a part of one could boost the credibility of your font designs.

The disadvantages were touched on above: potentially less profit, and (the flip side of letting the foundry control the business aspects for you) less control of business models and decisions, including sales venues and pricing. Also, an exclusive contract is, similarly, both liberating and constrictive at the same time.

HOW TO GET SIGNED

Now, how do you go about getting signed to a good foundry? There are three components: talent, connections, and luck.

Talent is, obviously, something that has two components to it: native ability and hard work. You'll need some of both to genuinely become a great font maker. All of the native ability in the world won't amount to anything if you don't spend the requisite number of hours actually drawing type and working with the tools of the trade. Similarly, you can work for thousands of hours, and if you don't have the native ability somewhere within you to draw something beautiful, your work won't amount to much. I personally believe that hard work is the far more important aspect of talent in font creation. Someone with a moderately good eye and a tremendous work ethic can create some fabulous fonts.

Connections in the world of fonts are important, especially if you have designs on signing with a major foundry. It's a relatively small community of typographers, and becoming a part of that community will be both enriching and politically savvy for you. Network through various social media (Twitter, the Typophile forums, and the iLoveTypography.com website are great places to start); get your work out there and accept critiques (and praise!); go to type conferences, classes, and camps.

If you are going to try to sign with a foundry, aim somewhere around your level of expertise and experience. Don't submit your first font to a major foundry and ask them to sign you. Release some fonts through your own foundry first, and try selling them on MyFonts.com or Fonts.com. Develop a portfolio and a style.

Web fonts

One of the prime typographic problems plaguing web design for years has been the usability of fonts. At first, even though there were ways to specify which fonts should be used in an HTML page, it all boiled down to what fonts your users had available to them. If you specified that your HTML paragraphs should display in Minion Pro, but a user visiting your site didn't have Minion Pro, then the page would not display the way you wanted.

Eventually, web developers came up with various mechanisms for actually delivering fonts from a web server to users' web browsers, meaning that if you specified Minion Pro in your web page, your server would feed that font to your visitors and display the page correctly, regardless of the fonts the visitors actually owned.

Naturally, this was a problem for many font developers. Serving a font over the web meant that people browsing a site could potentially download the font being served and use it for other purposes, thus providing an easy outlet for font piracy. To make a long story short, the technological issues have been sorted out by a slew of smart people, and web fonts are now usable and safe, for font developers and web browsers alike. The field has opened up a huge source of potential revenue for font developers, though it's not an uncontroversial thing—some font developers feel that web fonts will wind up cheapening the entire price structure for fonts, in the same way that iTunes has cheapened the pricing of music. Nonetheless, it's safe to say that web fonts are here to stay, and it's probably a good thing for you as a font creator to embrace.

ONLINE SERVICES

The major players right now are:

FontDeck
http://fontdeck.com
(You can read more about their policies for foundries here: http://fontdeck.com/about/foundries)

TypeKit (recently acquired by Adobe)
http://typekit.com
(Foundry info here: https://typekit.com/help/foundries)
Images 1–6 are screenshots from the web fonts gallery at TypeKit—not your average Georgia and Verdana!

Fonts.com
http://webfonts.fonts.com

MyFonts.com
http://new.myfonts.com/info/webfonts

Google
www.google.com/webfonts
(Foundry info at:
https://services.google.com/fb/forms/submitafont)

All of these services host web fonts on their own servers, so you as a foundry only have to submit your fonts to them and then you don't have to worry about any of the technical details.

If you're submitting your fonts for sale to MyFonts.com and Fonts.com, you can opt in to their web font service very easily, and this makes it a simple addition to your revenue stream. TypeKit and FontDeck are exclusively web-font sellers, which means you'd have to submit your fonts to them only for use as web fonts.

Google web fonts are all served up for free, so submitting your fonts to them is not a potential revenue stream. However, if you have any free fonts, it would be a good public relations move to have them served up by Google, so you should think about submitting them.

1

2

3

SERGIY TKACHENKO

Sergiy Tkachenko is an independent type designer from Kremenchuk, Ukraine.

He has been a practicing software programmer and designer since 1993. Living in Ukraine, where all the major languages use the Cyrillic script, his main priority in font development is the creation of multi-language typefaces that must contain the Cyrillic character set.

After trying out font design as a young man, Sergiy returned to developing fonts in 2007, selling his creations through MyFonts.

How did you decide to create fonts?

"It started when I was still a child. My father used to have a collection of ads and headline clippings from foreign magazines on culture, architecture, and painting. My first practical experience came when I was 11. Those were the last years of the Soviet Union and many new shops needed a good design. The very first fonts were stenciled, drawn on a paper roll, and cut out with knives made of broken hacksaws. I was trying out many things at that time: designing, programming, modeling ships and cars, and so on. One stencil was made for an inscription on a jib of an automobile crane.

When I was 16 my interest for design diminished and I was fully engaged in programming software. From 1997 to 2009 I was the head of an IT department of a local firm. I developed no new fonts but watched the market closely. In 2007 I decided to return to my old passion—developing fonts.

But since then many things have changed; first, I had to learn how to work with font editors. And there were many. It was then that I had an idea to offer my fonts via an online shop and chose MyFonts. I decided to start with a simple module font 3x3 with rounded angles. This is how I created Bladi One 4F, which went on sale in April 2008. During the whole of 2008, I studied font editors and developed two more fonts—Abia Wide 4F and Bladi Two 4F. They went on sale in December 2008 and were on a list in Hot News on MyFonts. It was a turning point. The more experienced I was, the more ideas I could put into practice."

Is it essential for a type designer to know a Cyrillic language to design Cyrillic fonts?

"Matthew Carter doesn't know a single language with Cyrillic writing, but he develops perfect Cyrillic versions of his fonts!"

> "THE MORE EXPERIENCED I WAS, THE MORE IDEAS I COULD PUT INTO PRACTICE."

Have you learned any lessons from creating fonts that you would share with a novice?

"I haven't studied the art of creating fonts. I have read no books about it, which might seem strange. All my knowledge comes from practical experience—trial and error. It is very important to analyze other fonts, both good and bad. Still, I highly recommend reading specialist literature."

What is your font creation process?

"I start drawing directly in FontLab. It is easier for me. In my work I use FontLab macros from BetaType (see http://betatype.com/taxonomy/term/4)."

Do you have any thoughts about the future of the font business?

"The font business must and will grow. I share the view of some designers who try to add as many languages as possible to their fonts. Web fonts have a great future. Using fonts on the web gives designers more freedom to realize their ideas. This is why it is important to have fonts supporting different languages, especially for brands wishing to go beyond a local market."

Do you remember the first time you saw a font of yours used on product packaging or a website? How did that feel?

"I first saw some of my fonts in a Ukrainian men's magazine, *Putt*. They used my fonts Boldesqo Serif 4F and Tovstun 4F for some short headlines and did a good job. My joy was overwhelming. It is a very special moment for a designer to see how your font is applied. I'm always very grateful to those customers who send me links and pictures of things with my fonts. The next font of mine I saw in action was Bladi Two 4F. It appeared on the cover of a Ukrainian news magazine, *Glavred*, for more than a year It is one thing to sell a license for a font and quite another to see it really working."

"ONE STENCIL WAS MADE FOR AN INSCRIPTION ON A JIB OF AN AUTOMOBILE CRANE."

"IT IS ONE THING TO SELL A LICENSE FOR A FONT AND QUITE ANOTHER TO SEE IT REALLY WORKING. "

sergiy tkachenko

1.

2.

3.

Bladi Two 4F
сучасна українська типографія
важка акциденція
але легко читається
власний стиль з м'якими вуглами
латинська діакритика
Регуляр, Конденсед, Стенсіл
широке коло застосування
найуспішніший проект

theGUnstore

оружейный магазин
космические просторы
можно увидеть на обложке
постоянная ширина знаков
милитаристический дизайн
большое число знаков
правильная цена

4.

ТРЕБА
ЕКОНОМНО
ВИКОРИСТОВУВАТИ
ПАПІР

Stenciliqo

Борец за идею Чочхэ
выступил с гиком, шумом,
жаром и фырканьем
на съезде — и в ящик.

1. Lavina 4F: a delicate, yet sturdy display font with lovely and interesting terminals.

2. Grotesqa 4F: a tall, bold font, great for setting at large sizes.

3. Bladi Two 4F: this has 22 members, from bold to stencil to condensed.

4. Stenciliqo 4F: comes with extruded family members.

5. Waldemar 4F: is a beautifully crafted high-contrast sans, with just a hint of a semi-serif.

5.

the quick brown fox jumps over the lazy dog

парубок
красна дівчина

сила воли, твердость характера, благородство и великодушие
Вальдемар

Жълтата дюля беше щастлива, че прхът, който цъфна, замръзна като гьон

stereo player

Kæmi nú öxi hér ykist þjófum nú bæði víl og ádrepa

На зеленій Україні

Pójdźże, kiń tę chmurność w głąb flaszy!

Vxskaftbud, ge vår wczonmö iqhjälp

Resources

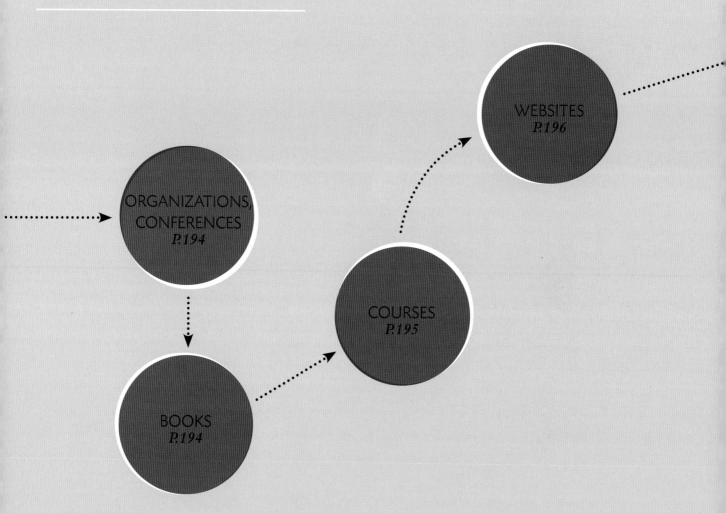

ORGANIZATIONS,
CONFERENCES
P.194

BOOKS
P.194

COURSES
P.195

WEBSITES
P.196

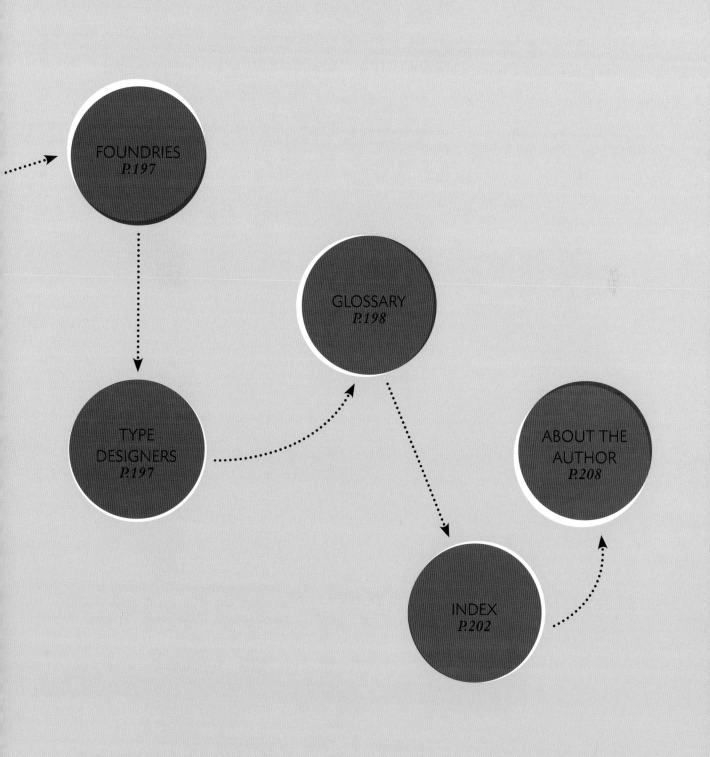

Books and websites

TYPOGRAPHY ORGANIZATIONS AND CONFERENCES

Ampersand Web Typography Conference
ampersandconf.com

UK-based annual conference dedicated to web typography.

ATypI (Association Typographique Internationale) Annual Conference
www.atypi.org

AtypI is the premier worldwide organization dedicated to type and typography. Its conference is held in a different country each year.

TypeCon (SOTA—The Society of Typographic Aficionados)
www.typecon.com / www.typesociety.org

Annual conference held in the USA and organized by SOTA.

Type Directors Club
typography. tdc.org

Leading international organization promoting excellence in typography.

TYPO Talks
www.typotalks.com

Type design conferences held in Europe and the USA.

TYPOGRAPHY BOOKS

The Complete Manual of Typography: A Guide to Setting Perfect Type.
Jim Felici. Adobe Press, 2011.

Updated edition of the seminal guide to type setting like a professional.

Designing Type.
Karen Cheng. Yale University Press, 2006.

A guide to creating and designing type, with information about the history of type.

The Elements of Typographic Style.
Robert Bringhurst. Hartley and Marks Publishers, 2004.

Combines practical, theoretical, and historical information about typographic style.

Handmade Type Workshop: Tips, Tools & Techniques for Creating Custom Typography.
Charlotte Rivers. HOW, 2011.

Tutorials teach the reader how to create and use original and customized letterforms.

Indie Fonts 3: A Compendium of Digital Type from Independent Foundries.
Richard Kegler, James Grieshaber, Tamye Riggs. Rockport, 2007.

Showcase of over 1,500 fonts from digital type foundries.

Stop Stealing Sheep & Find Out How Type Works.
Erik Spiekermann and E.M. Ginger. Adobe Press, 2002.

Classic typography book, updated to include information about web fonts.

Thinking with Type: A Critical Guide for Designers, Writers, Editors, and Students.
Ellen Lupton. Princeton Architectural Press, 2010.

A guide to using typography in visual communication, including information on font licensing and hand lettering

TYPOGRAPHY COURSES

Carrera de Diseño de Tipografía at
Universidad de Buenos Aires, Buenos Aires, Argentina
cdt-uba.org

Offers a one-and-a-half-year postgraduate course.

Cooper Union, New York City, USA
coopertype.org

The Continuing Education Department of The Cooper Union, in conjunction with the Type Directors Club, offers a Postgraduate Certificate in Typeface Design. The Extended Program in Typeface Design runs for three terms (fall, spring, and summer). A summer Intensive in Typeface Design runs from mid-June through mid-July.

Royal Academy of Art, The Hague, the Netherlands
www.kabk.nl/

Offers a postgraduate course in Type and Media, formerly the course in Type Design and Typography. It is a full-time one-year course that gives participants the possibility of delving deeper in type design for different media: not only type for print, but also for film, television, video, and interactive media.

Type Camp
typecamp.org

Courses on type design held at various international locations.

University of Reading, Reading, UK
www.reading.ac.uk/typography

For over 30 years, the Department of Typography & Graphic Communication at the University of Reading has been the only one of its kind in Britain. Offers an M.A. in Typeface Design.

FONT FACE INTERVIEW SUBJECTS

Aaron Bell
aaronb.net

Jos Buivenga
www.exljbris.com/

Emily Conners
new.myfonts.com/person/Emily_Conners/
www.dafont.com/emily-conners.d3353

Sergiy Tkachenko
www.4thfebruary.com.ua

TYPOGRAPHY WEBSITES

FontLab

www.fontlab.com

Official website for FontLab.

Fonts in Use

FontsInUse.com

Typography gallery, with work arranged by industry, format, and font.

Friends of Type

friendsoftype.com

Showcase for original typographic design and lettering.

Identifont

www.identifont.com

Online digital font directory.

I Love Typography

iLoveTypography.com

The premier website for general typographic knowledge and enthusiasm.

Majoor's Type Blog

www.martinmajoor.com/0_my_type_blog.html

Typography blog written by Dutch designer Martin Majoor.

The Ministry of Type

ministryoftype.co.uk

Blog about type, typography, lettering and calligraphy.

Monotype Imaging

www.monotypeimaging.com

Supplier of font and imaging software.

MyFonts

www.myfonts.com

The world's largest collection of fonts!

Nice Web Type

nicewebtype.com

Resources and tools for web type designers.

Typedia

typedia.com

A Wikipedia-style site documenting fonts, font designers, and foundries.

TypeDNA

www.typedna.com

Developer of font technologies and software.

Typographica

typographica.org

Includes reviews of typefaces and type books.

Typography Served

www.typographyserved.com

A gallery site featuring new typographic artwork, arranged by color.

Typojungle

typojungle.net

Online journal of visual culture, showcasing typography and graphic design.

Typophile

typophile.com

Home of the famous Typophile forums, where typographers and typography fans wax philosophical about all things type.

We Love Typography

weLoveTypography.com

Showcase of new typographic work.

FOUNDRIES AND TYPE DESIGNERS

4th February
fonts.4thfebruary.com.ua

Adobe
www.adobe.com/type

Ascender Fonts
www.ascenderfonts.com

CanadaType
canadatype.com

Chank Fonts
www.chank.com

Commercial Type
commercialtype.com

Dezcom
www.dezcom.com

DSType
www.dstype.com

Emigre
emigre.com

Erik Spiekermann
spiekermann.com

Exljbris
www.exljbris.com

Filmotype
www.filmotype.com

The Font Bureau
www.fontbureau.com

Font Deck
fontdeck.com

Font Fabric
fontfabric.com

FontFont
www.fontfont.com

Fonts
fonts.com

Fountain Type
www.fountaintype.com

H. Berthold Type Foundry
www.bertholdtypes.com

Hoefler & Frere-Jones
www.typography.com

House Industries
www.houseind.com

Hype for Type
www.hypefortype.com

Insigne
www.insignedesign.com

Jesse Ragan
www.jesseragan.com

Just Another Foundry
justanotherfoundry.com

Klim Type Foundry
klim.co.nz

Karsten Luecke Type Foundry
kltf.de

Laura Worthington
www.checkoutmyportfolio.com

The League of Moveable Type
www.theleagueofmoveabletype.com

LettError
www.letterror.com

Linotype
www.linotype.com

Mark Simonson Studio
www.ms-studio.com

Miller Type Foundry
www.millertype.com

Nick's Fonts
www.nicksfonts.com

P22
www.p22.com

Positype
www.positype.com

Process Type Foundry
processtypefoundry.com

Stone Type Foundry
www.stonetypefoundry.com

Storm Type Foundry
www.stormtype.com

Sudtipos
www.sudtipos.com

Typadelic
www.typadelic.com

Typefonderie
www.typofonderie.com

Typekit
typekit.com

Typerepublic
www.typerepublic.com

Type Supply
www.typesupply.com

The Type Studio
thetypestudio.com

Type Trust
typetrust.com

Typotheque
www.typotheque.com

Underware
www.underware.nl

URW++
urwpp.de

Glossary

Accent
A mark placed over, under, or through a character. These are used to indicate a difference in the way a character is pronounced.

Align
The process of lining up type using a base grid as a reference point.

Arm
A jutting, horizontal stroke.

Ascender
The imaginary line to which tall lowercase glyphs reach.

ASCII
The American Standard Code for Information Interchange. The industry standard system for encoding letters. The original ASCII specification encoded only uppercase letters. Subsequent specifications of ASCII and other systems, such as Unicode, can encode many more characters, although they are still limited.

Baseline
The imaginary line upon which the non-descending bottoms of glyphs sit.

Bézier curve
Mathematical equation used to describe the character shapes in digital typography. Bézier curves are used in vector fonts to make the characters scalable.

Bold font
A font drawn with thicker strokes than the regular version to give it a heavier appearance.

Brush script font
A type of script font based on an artisan sign-writing style, designed to look like it was drawn with a brush.

Calligraphic font
A typeface that appears to have been drawn with a pen or brush, imitating the look of traditional calligraphy.

Cap height
The imaginary line to which uppercase glyphs reach.

Composite glyphs
A glyph composed of two or more other glyphs, for example "À."

Contextual alternates
Like stylistic alternates, these are alternative glyphs. However, unlike stylistic alternates, contextual alternates are not used to make wholesale substitutions. They are used to substitute glyphs only in specific contexts.

Crossbar
A horizontal stroke placed neither at the top nor the bottom of a glyph, which joins two other strokes.

Descender
The part of a lowercase letter that descends below the baseline. The descender line is the imaginary horizontal line marking the lowest point of a descender.

Diagonal
A major diagonal stroke of a glyph.

Discretionary ligature
A combined set of glyphs that is not geometrically necessary (like a standard ligature), but is included in a font to be aesthetically interesting.

Display font
A type of font suited for use on items such as posters, signage, etc., rather than for large tracts of text.

Extended
A typeface with letterforms that are expanded horizontally while retaining their original height.

Extenders
The ascenders and descenders of letterforms.

Font family
A group of fonts based on one design, but featuring a variety of weights, widths, and angles.

Formal script font
A type of script font designed to look like a piece of skillfully crafted calligraphy.

Foundry
Historically, a type foundry was a place for the manufacture of metal type. In modern terms, it is a designer or company that creates and/or distributes digital typefaces.

Geometric fonts
A type of sans serif font with a clean aesthetic. The design is modeled on perfect geometric figures.

Glyph
A shape in the font editing software that represents a character, such as a letter, number, or symbol. A font is made up of a set of glyphs.

Grotesque font
A type of sans serif font designed to a stark, minimalist aesthetic. The name grotesque is believed to come from the reaction of type purists to these extremely plain fonts.

Handle
In FontLab, a handle is a control point used to manipulate a glyph.

Handwriting font
A type of script font that is based on the look of an individual's handwriting.

Hinting
The process of programming a font to display well at all sizes and resolutions on electronic devices.

Horizontal metrics
Measurements of a font's width, including sidebearings.

Humanist font
A type of sans serif font designed to have more delicate, "humanist" characteristics than a grotesque font, such as greater variations in stroke widths and oval shapes rather than circles.

Italic font
A font where the glyphs are slanted, usually at around 12° to the right. The glyphs are also flourished or otherwise artistically styled to distinguish them from the regular font.

Kerning
The process of providing instructions to a font on how to precisely handle the spacing between character pairs. This is used in addition to sidebearings to correct the spacing between problematic pairs.

Leading
The vertical distance from baseline to baseline.

Leg
A diagonal offshoot stroke of a glyph.

Ligature
Two letterforms joined together to create a single form, for example "fi." Also known as a standard ligature.

Lobe
A closed circular stroke in a glyph.

Modern font
A type of serif font that features a huge contrast between strokes, thin serifs, and perfectly vertical axes.

Monoline
A font line of consistent width.

Oblique font
Like an italic font, an oblique font is slanted usually at around 12° to the right, but does not have additional artistic styling.

Old style font
A type of serif font that features a non-vertical axis and has a low calligraphic contrast between its thicker and thinner strokes.

OpenType font
Digital font format developed jointly by Adobe and Microsoft. OpenType fonts are designed to work universally across platforms. OpenType fonts can contain more glyphs, support more languages, and can embed more professional typographic features than TrueType or Postscript fonts.

Outline font
A computer file containing the outline or vector information of a font; its set of character shapes are mathematically described by lines and curves. Outline fonts are scalable to any size. Also known as a scalable font.

Overshoot
The small amount a rounded part of a glyph generally extends above or below one of the usual vertical metrics (baseline, descender, ascender, x-height, or cap height).

Pixel
The smallest element of a digital image. Pixels are tiny, colored squares, which contain the basic mathematical information needed to determine the tone and color of an image. The greater the number of pixels per inch, the higher the resolution.

Point
The unit used to measure a font is called a point. In FontLab, a point also refers to the control point used to manipulate a glyph.

Point size
Measured in points, the point size is generally the height of the type's body.

Proportional lining numerals
These numerals have varying widths, all sit on the baseline, and reach to the same height line.

Proportional oldstyle numerals
These numerals have varying heights and sit at different vertical locations, mimicking varieties of lowercase letters.

Raster graphic
A bitmap image formed from a grid of pixels. Unlike vector graphics, raster images cannot be scaled up without losing image quality.

Regular font
See Roman font.

Reseller
A company that sells fonts from multiple type foundries/designers. The foundry/designer recieves a percentage of the retail price in exchange.

Roman font
The regular version of a typeface. Can also refer to fonts based on Ancient Roman lettering.

Sans serif
Letters without serifs. Sans serif fonts are generally used for shorter amounts of text, such as headlines, captions, and posters.

Scalable font
See Outline font.

Script fonts
A category of fonts where the characters are designed to appear as though they were drawn by hand. The look of these designs can range from informal handwriting to highly stylized, formal scripts. Script fonts are generally used for posters, signs, invitations, certificates, and packaging.

Serif
A small stroke at the top and bottom of a letter. Serif fonts are generally used for large tracts of text, such as a book or essay.

Sidebearings
The imaginary lines denoting the left and right boundaries of a glyph. Sidebearings tell software programs where a glyph begins and ends.

Slab serif font
A type of serif font that generally has very little contrast between the thick and thin strokes and has thick, rectangular serifs.

Slant angle
The slant angle of a font can be varied to introduce a new variant to a font family. For example, an italic font can be added by setting the characters to a slant angle of 12° to the right.

Small caps
Uppercase glyphs drawn at a lowercase scale, usually designed to be as tall as the font's x-height. Small caps are generally used for subheadings in blocks of text.

Spacing
The space, or the way space is arranged, between characters, words, and lines of type.

Spur
A type of finishing stroke used on some letterforms in some typefaces.

Standard ligature
See Ligature.

Stem
The major vertical stroke in a glyph.

Stroke
The main line or curve that forms a character.

Stylistic alternates
Alternative glyphs in a font to be used in special typographic circumstances and to add variety. They are generally applied as wholesale substitutes, applied to an entire paragraph of text, for example.

Swashes
Decorative versions of standard glyphs, often used at the beginnings of words or paragraphs.

Tabular lining numerals
These numerals take lining figures and create sidebearings around them that are all equal. This means that if they are used in a document with the kerning off, the numerals will line up in perfect vertical columns.

Tail
A downward projection on a character.

Terminal
The end of a stroke, often designed to be decorative. Types of terminals include serifs, spurs, and tails.

Tracking
The letterspacing in a font. Most typesetting software can tighten or loosen the tracking in small increments.

Transitional font
A type of serif font that has a greater contrast between thicker and thinner strokes and a more vertical axis than an old-style font.

TrueType font
Outline font format developed by Apple, but can also be used with Windows. TrueType fonts can be used for both screen and print.

Type 1 Postscript font
Outline font format developed by Adobe and designed to communicate smoothly with Postscript printers. Postscript fonts can be used on multiple platforms.

Unicode
A standard developed to represent (or encode) letters of alphabets so that they can be transmitted and decoded by computers. Unicode can encode over a million characters, however, even so it is limited when you consider non-Latin languages such as Cyrillic, Greek, Arabic, and Hebrew, and languages such as Chinese, Japanese, and Korean, which have large numbers of characters including pictograms, ideograms, and semantic-phonetic compounds, and historic scripts and obsolete characters that scholars might use.

Vector graphic
Graphic format that uses mathematical calculations to reproduce lines and curves on screen. When an image is scaled up, the calculations are redone so that the image displays without image degradation.

Vertical metrics
The measurements of a font's height. The five most important vertical metrics are the baseline, ascender, descender, x-height, and cap height.

Weight
The measurement of a stroke's width. Most font families include several weights, such as light, regular, and bold.

Width
The most commonly used widths in a font family are narrow (also known as condensed), regular, and extended (also known as wide). A narrow font is compressed horizontally, while an extended font is expanded horizontally.

X-height
The imaginary line to which normal height lowercase glyphs reach.

Index

About the Author

Alec Julien is a font creator and graphic designer living in the northeastern United States. He started his own font foundry, Haiku Monkey, in 2007, and has since published over 50 font families, including two open source families, and nearly four dozen for sale on MyFonts.com and Fonts.com. He has published typography articles online on his own blog and on the renowned iLoveTypography.com, touching on a wide range of topics, from practical matters of font creation, to ligatures in graffiti, to the ephemeral topic of analyzing inconspicuous vertical metrics.